going on retreat

going on retreat

a beginner's guide to the
christian retreat experience

margaret silf

LOYOLAPRESS.

CHICAGO

LOYOLAPRESS.

3441 N. ASHLAND AVENUE
CHICAGO, ILLINOIS 60657

Published in Great Britain in 2002 as *Soul Space: Making a Retreat in the Christian Tradition*
Society for Promoting Christian Knowledge
Holy Trinity Church
Marylebone Road
London NW1 4DU

Interior design by Kathy Kikkert
Cover images courtesy of: (top left) Christopher Fuller, San Damiano Retreat, Danville, CA, (bottom right) Tom Grant, San Damiano Retreat, Danville, CA, (bottom left) Bellarmine Hall, Barrington, IL.

Library of Congress Cataloging-in-Publication Data

Silf, Margaret.
  Going on retreat: a beginner's guide to the Christian retreat experience / Margaret Silf.
     p. cm.
Includes bibliographical references.
  ISBN 0-8294-1994-2
 1. Spiritual retreats. I. Title.
 BV5068.R4 S57 2002
 269'.6—dc21

2002003598

Printed in the United States of America
02 03 04 05 Bang 10 9 8 7 6 5 4 3 2 1

about the author

Formerly employed in the computer industry, Margaret Silf has been trained by the Jesuits to accompany others in prayer. She is now engaged full-time in writing, in facilitating retreats and days of reflection, and in being a companion to others on their spiritual journeys. Born and brought up in Yorkshire, Margaret now lives in Staffordshire. She is married and has one daughter. She is an ecumenical Christian, committed to working across and beyond denominational boundaries.

Margaret is the author of *2001: A Book of Grace-Filled Days* and its sequel, *2002; Inner Compass: An Invitation to Ignatian Spirituality;* and *Close to the Heart: A Guide to Personal Prayer* (all with Loyola Press, Chicago); *The Miller's Tale and Other Parables* (Darton, Longman and Todd); *Wayfaring: A Gospel Journey into Life* (Doubleday); and *Sacred Spaces: Stations on a Celtic Way* (Paraclete).

contents

INTRODUCTION *ix*

CHAPTER ONE
Why Should I Make a Retreat? 1

CHAPTER TWO
What Is a Residential Retreat? 25

CHAPTER THREE
Can I Still Make a Retreat if I Can't Get Away? 57

CHAPTER FOUR
Retreat Companions, Prayer Guides, and Soul Friends 79

CHAPTER FIVE
How Should I Prepare for My Retreat Experience? 113

CHAPTER SIX
I'm Here! Now What? 135

CHAPTER SEVEN
Keeping the Retreat Experience Alive 161

CHAPTER EIGHT
The Spiritual Exercises of St. Ignatius of Loyola 173

APPENDIX ONE
Retreat Centers in the United States 191

APPENDIX TWO
Suggested Reading 198

introduction

Scripture tells us that Jesus frequently retreated to be alone with his Father. At times of major decision, he spent extended periods of time in the silence of the hills, discerning his way forward. This model alone should be enough to encourage those of us who bear his name to follow his example.

The quest for enlightenment

Mystics of every faith tradition have engaged in what we might call the quest for enlightenment. This sounds rather pompous, otherworldly, and irrelevant to us who have to live our lives very solidly *in* the world. Yet "enlightenment" is what enables us to see where we are going and what we are about; it gives us the energy we need to get on with our living.

I experienced this kind of everyday enlightenment in a particularly vivid way early one morning while vacationing on a Mediterranean island. My watch buried under all the "necessities" I had thought I would need, I became more aware of the natural rhythms of the day. As the days passed, I was reminded of how healing and restoring it can be to exchange the time-tabled world for the natural cycles of dawn, day, dusk, and darkness. Each morning the rising sun exercised its power to penetrate my slumber with a determination stronger than my natural laziness. The noonday sun compelled a siesta. The lengthening shadows of evening set the night music going and released a cooler energy. The nonnegotiable dark of a near-desert night poured an infusion of silence into the cocktail of life.

Each morning I began to look forward to the moment when the tiniest gleam of gold would appear at the summit of the hills beyond my bedroom window. In that instant, it seemed to me as though some divine finger would strike a match, creating light and fire for all the ages still to come. Then, ever so gradually, the light would flow down the hillside and flood the valley, bringing a whole new day to life. It was a daily miracle.

As I remember this Mediterranean sunrise, I can think of neither a simpler nor a more potent expression of enlightenment than to greet the dawn with an expectant awareness and to let its life-giving energy tumble through every crevasse of life on earth. By making a retreat, we are seeking something of this enlightenment for our own living. We are climbing to a hilltop place, in a sense, and seeking to remove ourselves from our everyday concerns for a while. We are allowing God to illuminate the deeper recesses of our minds and hearts; we are letting his presence flow from that encounter into the plains and valleys of our everyday lives.

Enlightenment, of course, does not depend on remote mountaintops or Mediterranean dawns. Nor are we required to take extended time from our normal routines or go to any complicated or expensive efforts. However we choose to do it, the purpose is the same: to reflect upon the ways God's energy may be active in our living. I hope that this book will open up some possibilities for stepping aside to make time for God, however briefly, in ways that you may perhaps not have considered before.

Using this book

If you feel drawn to the idea of making a retreat, I hope that this book will encourage you in a number of ways:

• In chapter 1, we consider some of the reasons people decide to make a retreat. We take a look at some of the benefits to the whole person, body and soul.

• In chapter 2, we consider various types of retreats available in order to help you determine what type might appeal to you and suit your personal circumstances. This section offers a brief overview of various types of retreats and the kind of guidance or companionship you might expect from each.

• Chapter 3 offers helpful suggestions for those who would like to make a retreat, but for whom it is impossible to get away from daily life for extended periods. This section also provides guidance to those who have never made a retreat before, to help them to prepare for the occasion.

• Chapter 4 provides some insights into the kind of relationship you can expect to have with your retreat companion or prayer guide, and how this differs from "soul friendship" or spiritual direction.

• Chapter 5 offers suggestions to help you prepare for the retreat you have selected, including many practical considerations to guide your preparations.

• In chapter 6, we take a look at what you will probably find when you arrive at your retreat. In this section we also consider how to handle the inevitable distractions that will arise, particularly interior distractions.

• Chapter 7 provides a number of suggestions for sustaining the benefits of your retreat experience and for making a smooth transition back into your daily routine.

• In chapter 8, we explore one of the best-known of all spiritual retreats, the Spiritual Exercises of St. Ignatius of Loyola. We will look at both the residential, monthlong retreat form and the more extended (and for many, more manageable) daily-life "Nineteenth Annotation."

• The book concludes with a resource section that will help you find the kind of retreat you want, in the venue you will find most helpful. It also provides some guide-lines for those who wish to organize a group retreat.

A word of thanks . . .

. . . to so many people who have helped in the shaping of this book.

My special thanks go to Kerry Hiscock for her invaluable insights, her searching questions and comments, and her tireless patience in reading and rereading the draft of the UK edition; to Paddy Lane of the Retreat Association for all her support and encouragement and the information and advice she has so generously provided; to Breda Gainey, Gerry Hughes, and Michael Ivens for their generosity in taking time to read and comment on the draft of the UK edition; to those who so kindly contributed their firsthand accounts of the experience of making a retreat.

A book that claims to offer an introduction to what it means to make a retreat is necessarily subjective and inevitably based on the author's own, limited, experience. I hope that this book will encourage the hesitant to make a retreat, if they feel so drawn, and that it may open up a few new possibilities for those who are more experienced in making retreats.

The book was originally written as a guide to retreat making in the United Kingdom and was based upon the practices and perceptions of retreat making and retreat giving that are current in the United Kingdom. The adaptation of this material to make it appropriate to

American readers has been undertaken by Heidi Saxton, who has carried out substantial revision and major restructuring of the original material (published by the Society for Promoting Christian Knowledge in the United Kingdom under the title *Soul Space*) to this end. I would like to thank Heidi for her considerable work in this respect and for her perseverance both in resolving issues arising from differences between the U.K. and the U.S. approaches to making a retreat and in researching the U.S. equivalents to the facilities described in the U.K. edition of the book. My thanks also go to Rebecca Johnson of Loyola Press, who has overseen the transition of the material from a U.K. to a U.S. readership.

It is impossible to give due thanks to the many, many people who contribute to the wealth of retreat opportunities now available. However, my special personal thanks go to my Jesuit friends Gerry Hughes and Michael Ivens (who have pioneered the growth of Ignatian retreats in the United Kingdom, and made them accessible to lay people, and in daily life), Fintan Creavan, Brian McClorry, Damian Jackson, Tom McGuinness and Paul Nicholson, all who work alongside them, and all who have accompanied my own retreats.

To all who have sown the seeds of prayer in our time and place, we who reap the fruits thank you, and thank God.

why should i make a retreat?

THERE'S SOMETHING ABOUT the word *retreat* that can either set our hearts leaping at the prospect of making one or make us run a mile from the very idea. For some people, the word resonates with memories of school retreats that they either loved or hated. For others, it sounds like something exclusively for "holy people," however we understand that term. And yet, for each of us this simple word can touch upon deep longings for space, time, and solitude.

Most of us make some kind of retreat nearly every day of our lives. A harassed mother slips off to the bathroom in order to sit in uninterrupted peace for five minutes behind a locked door. An exhausted bus driver takes the dog for an evening walk in the park. A child hides away in a secret den in the loft, where her siblings can't find her, while she mulls over her feelings about a problem at school. All of these are little retreats, and from this deep instinctive need for space and peace we can begin to notice what actually makes a retreat and what we are looking for when we make one.

A LITTLE BACKGROUND ABOUT RETREATS

The first (and for some, the only) retreat experiences some people have are the annual retreats that are part of the curricula of many parochial schools. On the whole, these are "preached retreats." People assemble in large groups to hear a speaker—usually a priest—discuss a particular subject and then disperse to think over what they have heard. And even these kinds of retreats are not a memory shared by the large majority, most of whom attended public schools.

Thirty years ago, it would not have occurred to most laypeople to make a retreat. Retreats were for nuns and priests, and even then, "preached retreats" were the norm. They were times set aside for special instructions, as it were, to focus their minds in particular ways.

Then a sea change occurred. Beginning in North America, but rapidly spreading to the United Kingdom, enthusiasm began to gather for what has become known as the individually given retreat (or IGR). At first, these too were offered mainly by priests and mainly for the benefit of clergy and those in religious orders. However, in a relatively short time the possibility of making such a retreat was opened up to all Christians, and indeed to those of other faiths and of none.

This vision has led to the emergence of a large number of retreat houses, some with just a couple of rooms and some with over a hundred, where retreatants can spend time in reflective stillness, with a trained companion available to them if they so desire.

Now, therefore, it is very common for those making retreats to be laypeople, and even people who are not attached to any institutional church. There is a radical equality at the "oasis" of retreat space. The bishop might be in the room next to a clerk or coal miner. The retreat guide may also be a layperson, from any walk of life, of either gender. In a retreat in daily life, it is even more likely that the majority of retreatants and most of the prayer companions/prayer guides will be laity.

You will probably not know anything about the church background or status of your fellow retreatants, especially now when priests or those in religious orders rarely wear distinctive dress, at least not during their time in retreat. These superficial distinctions truly become irrelevant where all are making a journey, in their own way, to the very core of their being.

"What are the essential elements of a retreat?"

How can we turn ordinary time into *graced* time that can renew, challenge, and redirect us? Some suggestions might be:

• *A change of place.* For a short period, we withdraw from our routine activities. We may do this by physically going to a different place or by creating an oasis wherever we happen to be. One way to do this is to make a change in the environment where we usually spend our time, such as dedicating one corner of a room as a special place for prayer.

• *A change of pace.* Our "oasis time" is time spent apart from the normal noise of our daily activities. We may begin by switching off the external sounds of radio or TV. With practice, we can also learn the art of switching off the constant noise in our own heads in order to enjoy a bit of stillness. We become physically still, and we also cease our constant inner busyness for a while. In this deeper stillness, we begin to glimpse what is happening at the deepest levels of our being, at the heart of ourselves where our deepest feelings and highest visions begin to show themselves.

• *A change of focus.* As we relax our bodies, we also begin gradually to relax our hold on the personal anxieties of the day, making room for the wider world. Perspective lengthens as we come to stillness. We begin to see ourselves as parts of a greater whole, and we draw strength and peace in that reassurance. This larger perspective leads us back to the demands of everyday life with a more balanced view. We have dipped into a deeper layer of our own psyches, and sometimes we will find solutions and new directions that escape us while we are living in the cut and thrust of the daily struggle to survive.

A retreat is always a spiritual experience, whether or not we consider ourselves "spiritual." A retreat takes us closer to the core of our beings and to a space in which we also touch the reality of God. Kerry, a widow who spends much time alone, was delighted to discover this fact after being invited to go on a silent weekend retreat:

Before I went, I had been really fearful of the expected silence from Friday evening to Sunday afternoon, but I found it calming, peaceful, and friendly and not at all oppressive. Before I booked I had wondered to myself: "What do you take into a retreat? What do you take away from it?" Now I know the answers. I took into that retreat someone who was tired, tense, and nervous. When I left (reluctantly) two days later, I was calmer, happier, refreshed, and surer of my faith. What I had feared was going to be difficult turned out to be gold—God's gold! I would recommend it to anyone.

FIRST THINGS FIRST: COMMON QUESTIONS ABOUT THE RETREAT PROCESS

Almost everyone finds it daunting to think of making a formal retreat for the first time. The possibility raises a whole range of questions, from "What will it be like?"

through "What if I don't like what I'm hearing?" A little solid knowledge of what retreats are about and how they work can go a long way in encouraging us to make the venture. I explore the process in this book in the hope of addressing some of your questions and of shedding light on some of the many different types of retreat and what can be expected of them.

What kinds of retreats are available?

There are two primary types of retreats: residential and daily-life retreats.

Residential retreats, which involve spending time away from home for the duration of the retreat, are available in a number of different forms. We will discuss some of the most common types more fully in chapter 2. For the present, let us identify two of the most common:

• *Theme retreats,* which can run from a weekend to six or eight days or more, are usually centered around a particular spiritual topic or theme. Although some of these retreats may be conducted mainly or partially in silence, most are structured around a series of talks or other group activities, with various opportunities for quiet reflection. The theme retreat is often the first type of residential retreat chosen by inexperienced retreatants.

• *Individually given retreats* (IGRs; sometimes called "individually guided retreats") are retreats that are almost always conducted in silence, during which a retreatant shares his or her experience in daily meetings with a prayer guide (or retreat companion). The purpose and role of this companion is explained in chapter 4. In an IGR, each retreatant sets his or her own daily schedule (apart from mealtimes and daily meetings with the companion). However, each retreatant is encouraged to plan his or her own time to include prayer, rest, and relaxation.

Daily-life retreats are especially valued by those unable to get away from home for any length of time. Some people prefer to make their first retreat experience a daily-life retreat. This involves committing to a daily time of prayer for a specific number of weeks or even months, with periodic meetings with a retreat companion or spiritual director.

If you are making a retreat for the first time (either in daily life or in a residential setting), your prayer companion/guide will be able to offer you extra guidance on how to get the best out of your retreat. Since this approach to retreat making is growing in popularity, you will find that many people making a retreat in daily life are doing so for the first time.

Are retreat houses run primarily for the benefit of people from a particular denomination? Will I feel out of place if I'm from a different denomination?

The simple answer is also an ambiguous one. It is probably true that most retreat houses are run by people who belong to a particular Christian denomination. When retreat houses advertise, many of them will indicate which denomination runs their center. However, it is also true that the great majority of retreat houses are also actively ecumenical in their approach and attitude. This is because, in its deeper reaches, prayer is always ecumenical; it takes us to the depths of our being, to places that lie well below the walls that appear to divide us. Retreat houses are primarily about the prayer that unites us, not the doctrines that divide us.

In the United States, many of the retreat houses are from either the Roman Catholic or the Anglican (Episcopalian) traditions, and they conduct their worship and other activities in line with these denominations. This means that in Episcopalian worship, Anglican Eucharist will be celebrated; in a Roman Catholic retreat house, the daily or Sunday Eucharist will take the form of a Catholic Mass.

In most residential retreats there will be a mix of Christians from all traditions. After a short time in retreat among others who are seeking God as you are yourself, you will forget about the divisions of name or doctrine or practice that still come between us in the outside world and feel increasingly at one with them in the deeper quest for God in our lives and in our world.

Will I be expected to know the Bible?

Normally a retreat guide will expect nothing from retreatants except openness toward making a journey of discovery and discernment of the ways in which God is acting in their lives. Whatever kind of retreat you are making, the retreat guide will normally not expect any particular familiarity with the Bible. If he or she uses Scripture during the retreat, perhaps in the course of the talks or as a focus for personal prayer in the quiet time, any necessary references will be clearly given.

Frequently, an IGR will involve the use of Scripture. If your guide suggests focusing your prayer on particular passages, he or she will tell you where and how to find them. In this kind of Scripture-based prayer, it is important to allow the words of Scripture, or the events of the Gospel and other scriptural stories, to touch *your own lived experience.*

Scripture can become a gateway to a personal encounter with God, and whether or not you are familiar with the structure and contents of the Bible is far less important than your openness to allowing Scripture to reveal connections between your own life and the Word of God. If you have a favorite version of the Bible, it may be helpful to take it with you on retreat. If biblical references are suggested, don't panic if you don't know where to start looking for them. Bibles always have a list of contents at the front, and many of us need to use it.

One of the most moving experiences I have ever had was while I was accompanying someone on an individually given retreat in daily life. At the end of our first meeting I suggested a couple of references that this person might like to look at and meditate with. The next week, the retreatant told me, very honestly, that he had not even known the difference between the Old and the New

Testaments, but that he had managed to find the psalms I had suggested by using the table of contents. As the retreat progressed, I discovered that this person was being drawn into very deep and life-changing prayer, and that he was powerfully affected by the connections he was finding between Scripture and his own experience. Some of God's closest friends have never "read the book"!

Will I be required to talk or pray in front of a group?

No. A sensitive retreat leader will not force anyone to participate in a group discussion or engage in vocal prayer, unless they so desire. Even in the context of a prayer service, people may be invited to voice their intentions aloud, but are never compelled to do so.

What if I'm not a practicing Christian? Will I still be welcome?

Certainly! All that is necessary in order for you to feel at home is that you yourself should feel comfortable knowing that the house where you will be staying is a Christian one.

Of course, if you have no allegiance to the Christian faith and do not sympathize with what we might call the Christic vision of life, then you might find that a theme retreat that is focused on a particular aspect of Christian faith or practice would not speak to you. There are, however, many theme retreats that look at issues beyond the traditional boundaries of Christian faith, and you might find one of these both interesting and challenging.

If you are not a Christian but decide to make an individually given retreat in a Christian retreat house, you will probably have made your position known in advance. Your retreat guide will be more than happy to be alongside you wherever you are. The guide's task would not be to convert you, the pilgrim, but rather to accompany you and to share the delights and the difficulties of your particular journey, whatever they happen to be.

We will explore the role of the retreat companion more fully in chapter 4. For now, let us simply say that guide and pilgrim meet as peers, fellow travelers on a spiritual journey. The absence of a commonly held creed or doctrinal base should make no difference to this process, which is conducted in mutual respect. Many of the retreat guides I know personally would be delighted to have the privilege of walking alongside a pilgrim of another faith during a retreat. Whether you are a practicing Christian or not, whether you go to church every day or haven't been inside a church since the last family wedding, makes absolutely no difference to the welcome and the acceptance you can expect from any type of retreat.

> *If I am struggling with a problem,*
> *will my retreat guide advise me*
> *on the best course of action?*

Most of us find ourselves, at some stage in our lives, grappling with some difficulty that begins to wear us down, leaving us feeling helpless and in need of a solution or resolution.

Solutions, however, are not what a retreat is about. A retreat is, first and foremost, about space and time. Such space and time may enable us to reflect on the implications of a problem in our lives. It may even give us the opportunity to share something of our feelings and our struggle, if we wish it, with a listener who will offer us nonjudgmental empathy. However, a retreat companion will *not* provide us with a fix or attempt to solve problems or offer therapy. There are several reasons for this, one of the most important being that most authentic solutions to personal problems are those we discover for ourselves.

And yet, we may find that our time of retreat has given us a new focus, a perspective that goes beyond ourselves to include others. The brief withdrawal may help us to recognize a way of coping with a difficult colleague, or more effective ways of expressing our feelings to our families, or a practical way of engaging the struggle to shape a more just society. These small but very significant changes of viewpoint and attitude are typical of what happens in a retreat, whether that retreat is a sustained period of silence in a retreat house or just a few minutes of quiet reflection on a busy day.

If I go on this retreat, am I just running away from my problems?

As adults, we sometimes begin to question our motives for making a retreat. We may wonder whether we just want to avoid the demands of our normal lives. If we don't question this for ourselves, there will probably be others who will question it for us. This accounts for some of the awkwardness we sometimes feel about taking time out to explore the deeper significance of our lives. It is important to remind ourselves that, rather than running away from our problems, we are turning our hearts in the direction of new solutions.

Initially, it is true, these brief withdrawals from the daily routine are a reaction to pressure. We withdraw *from* the routine, seeking a space for stillness. Once that stillness is discovered, however, we find that it contains a treasure that is indeed worth retreating *for.* That treasure may be the deepened perspective we gain or the new balance we find that enables us to return to daily life more creatively.

"What is the optimum length of time to spend in retreat?"

How long is a piece of string?

Seriously, the answer to this question depends entirely upon the person making the retreat and his or her particular needs at that time.

An individually given retreat does have a certain dynamic, partially reflected in the typical five-, six-, or eight-day duration. People often find that it can take two or three days to settle into a retreat. It is surprisingly difficult to switch off to all that was going on in our normal daily life before we came away on retreat. The first couple of days are used for winding down and, for many people, catching up on much-needed rest and relaxation. During these first days, a retreatant may be overconcerned with such questions as "What am I going to make of this retreat? What is its shape going to be?" When we stop worrying about these things, God gets a word in edge-wise, and the real issues begin to emerge.

Often it is the third, fourth, and fifth days when these issues come up in prayer and in your conversations with the guide. The third and fourth day can be difficult, especially if the retreat doesn't seem to be "going anywhere" in a way that the retreatant can readily recognize. Intensive prayer, as in an individually given retreat, also takes energy, and a certain spiritual exhaustion can show itself if the retreatant is not pacing him- or herself. The last day or two should focus on the gradual gathering of the fruits of the retreat and preparation for the return home.

If you are making an IGR in order to be open before God about serious issues in your life, you will probably benefit most from remaining in retreat at least five or six days. If you can spare eight days, this will give you more time to reflect on the key issues before preparing to return home.

If you wish to participate in a theme retreat, the optimum time is whatever time you can spare. A weekend is fine, and so is a week. The purpose of such a retreat is to nourish and encourage you along your journey.

"Isn't making a retreat a rather spartan experience?"

If we look back into history and reflect on how the early monks retreated or on how Jesus himself withdrew without food or water into the hills to come closer to the Father, we might well ask ourselves how so many of our modern retreat houses have come to be so comfortable.

Retreat houses, like most other things, come in all styles and degrees of comfort. In any retreat situation, you can expect to enjoy the privacy of a single room unless it is stated otherwise when you place your reservation. Probably the most significant factor that makes us feel at ease in a retreat house has less to do with the physical comforts it offers than with the atmosphere of warmth and acceptance that prevails there.

However, it is true that most retreat houses are warm and comfortable, both physically and psychologically. The nearest you will get to asceticism is a certain simplicity. A simply appointed retreat house will provide you with a small bedroom, often with its own sink and towel rack; a small closet for hanging your clothes; and maybe a book-shelf, a chair, and a little desk or writing area. Toilet and shower facilities will usually be close by and are usually shared with several other retreatants. Meals will often be buffet style, simple yet satisfying and varied. Vegetarian options are offered by most retreat centers.

To minimize overhead costs, some retreat houses ask retreatants to help a little with daily chores. You may be expected to help in the kitchen on occasion or strip and remake your bed when you leave. Most retreat houses provide an information sheet that outlines the house schedule, the house expectations, and how your room should be left at your departure.

At the other end of the comfort scale you will find retreat houses that offer spacious rooms, sometimes with a private bath, and more food than you could possibly eat. There may be other luxuries too, such as a Jacuzzi, massage, aromatherapy, reflexology, and so on.

Is fasting part of making a retreat?

The subject of fasting as a spiritual exercise is beyond the scope of this book. Suffice it to say that no retreat house would ever assume that you are intending to fast while on retreat, though some retreatants do want to do so for at least part of the time. Sometimes this intention fades once the retreatant sees the delicious provisions being offered!

Hospitality is an important part of the ministry of retreat giving. The house itself offers a warm welcome and a comfortable place to sleep, eat, pray, gather, and enjoy recreation. Your retreat guide offers a listening heart and a place where you can be truly yourself without fear of disapproval or diminishment. These are all ways in which God's love can be revealed, so you might want to think twice before entering into a strict fast while on retreat.

If you do decide to miss one or more meals throughout your retreat, avoid wasting food by letting the house administrator know in advance which meals you intend to skip. Some houses have a checklist for each day on which you can indicate an anticipated absence from a meal. Take care before entering upon a strict fast, either in retreat or out of it, and seek medical advice as appropriate. As to whether fasting is most likely to help or hinder your prayer on a given retreat, this may again be an appropriate topic of conversation with your prayer guide.

MEETING GOD IN DAILY LIFE

Making time for God need not be a complicated process. On the contrary, it can be as simple as taking a moment to gaze at the world, to see it with God's eyes. In doing so, we may be taken by surprise many times in the course of a single day: when we watch a sleeping child, for example, or notice the steady breathing of a loved one; when we see how the cobwebs on the downspout have turned to lace under the touch of frost, or notice one drop of dew on a rose petal. All of these are moments of retreat. They are all visits to the oasis in the depths of our hearts, where God is at home.

These moments happen when we go "out of ourselves" and allow God to speak to our hearts. Often, he does this through his creation. We cannot manufacture these occasions; we can only experience them. They flow with their own natural rhythms, taking us into an invisible world in which time ceases to drive us. They draw us into our own rhythms, rhythms that we may feel we have completely lost under the pressures of competitive living.

These moments energize us. We might find it hard to describe just how this energizing happens, but we can feel its effects. We come away from our times at the oasis with a renewed vitality and, perhaps, a deeper insight into the heart of things. It brings to life a whole new day in us. It flows right down into the valleys of our lives, changing the way we see things, making new things possible, opening up new pathways and views.

All of these are features of a retreat, whether it takes place in half an hour of stillness in a quiet spot or lasts for days or even months in the cloistered silence of a retreat house. Ordinary time is suspended to make a little space for eternity to reveal itself. The rhythm of our living begins to align itself with the natural rhythms of light and darkness, activity and rest. In ways we need not understand, we find new energy in the process and return to our routine enabled to live from a greater depth than before.

The purpose of this book is to open up some of the ways in which we can help this to happen. It suggests some ways of taking time out to experience the deeper sources of our being. These include the traditional ways of making a retreat in a secluded environment as well as the increasingly accessible ways of making a retreat within the routine of our daily lives. All are ways of being at the oasis, of going to the well of living water that is always there for us. They invite us to pause the video of our busyness long enough to draw from that eternal well.

RETREATING *FROM* OR RETREATING *FOR*?

For many people, the entire spiritual journey, including all personal prayer, is open to the charge of unhealthy introspection. So we must ask ourselves what we are actually doing when we attempt to move inward to the core (or the "ground") of our being. Is this attempt to come closer to God drawing us further away from each other? Is it a narcissistic spirituality, and if so, can this have anything to do with the kingdom of God?

I have grappled with this question myself, and I remain convinced that when we go deep into the heart of ourselves, we also come closer to the heart of each other. In prayer, and especially in the intensive prayer of a retreat, we go down, as it were, to the bedrock of our own being. To delve into the core of our own being is also to dig into that bedrock where we are mysteriously in touch with the core of all being—the place where all is one. The evidence for the truth of this lies in the effects it has: if we return to the everyday world after prayer more in harmony with creation and with all other beings, then the encounter at the bedrock has been creative in ways that will radiate outward and be life-giving for others as well as for ourselves.

If this is so, then to make a retreat is not to escape from the real world, but to be in touch with aspects of reality that are often covered over with noise and busyness. We open ourselves up to our interrelatedness and see afresh anything that is blocking this wholeness. If we really start to do this, we may begin to realize that things are the other way around: we are often "escaping" from reality when we are so busy doing all the things we find so important in daily life, and we are facing and encountering a deeper reality when we take time to be still and to listen to the movements of our hearts.

If prayer, meditation, and sustained times of retreat enable us to move closer to the core of our own being and to the core of all being, this movement has a purpose. We are empowered in the depths of this core to move *out* again with renewed energy and vision, to turn our contemplation into action within a wounded world, and to make choices and decisions that will contribute to our world's healing.

Keeping "Mum" before God

Here is one woman's story of her retreat experience.

Life as the mother of two small children is always wonderful, but it can be exhausting. There are times, too, especially when the children are very small and at home full-time, that Mom's very identity (the one before "Mom"!) seems to disappear beneath the diapers, picture books, and Lego toys. We wouldn't be human if we didn't sometimes cry, "There must be more to life than this." So when a friend asked me to go to a retreat with her, I didn't hesitate. My enormously supportive husband can manage perfectly well without me—he pushed me out of the house with instructions to rest and enjoy.

A retreat can be restful, but it can also provide refreshment through challenge. It wasn't an easy weekend. Going from the busyness of family life to retreat (especially a silent one, as this was) was a difficult transition. It was wonderful to eat a lovely meal without having to cook or wash up, but it took a while to let go. It was helpful to have someone to direct the retreat who could move my thoughts away from the mundane.

The countryside around the retreat house was lovely, and I enjoyed being able to walk at a grown-up pace and in silence. The retreat house is situated near a racetrack, and the sound of speeding motors prompted me to pray for the world I'd retreated from. In the absence of constant toddler voices, I found myself surprised—even disturbed—by God. I told him that I wanted more out of life. Gracious and merciful, he even let me shout at him (and yes, I did shout, even though it was a silent retreat!). I was well out of earshot and felt thoroughly released by it; with that out of my system, it was easier for me to listen to God. At the end of the lovely garden is a cross, and there God spoke to me.

I thought that I needed something new, something that would restore "my" identity. Instead, God challenged and strengthened me to persevere with the task in hand. The retreat helped me to live in the now and not in the "I wish"; it also allowed God to parent me. By the end, I was aching to get back to my daughters and husband, to get back to the task that really is "me." So on a sunny Sunday afternoon, I drove home to my family, ready to go on with the best job in the world—being a mom.

The fruits of retreat

As Christians, we know that Jesus himself would frequently withdraw to a quiet place to pray. His model is an invitation to us to do the same in whatever ways we can. We also know that withdrawing into seclusion from time to time has always been a valued part of the Christian tradition. This seems to have been especially

important at times of great trial or at times when the
light of the gospel values seemed to be dimming. Yet Jesus
himself tells us, "By their fruits you shall know them," and
I believe we can—and must—apply this test to our
retreating. If it bears good fruit for ourselves, for those
around us, and for all creation, then it is of God. If it iso-
lates us from others and from the needs of the world,
then it is not of God. Each of us must discern this for
ourselves.

However, a time of seclusion may bear fruit that does
not immediately and obviously translate into new external activities. At times we need refreshment, renewal, and
nurturing in order to meet our normal responsibilities
with our families and friends, jobs, or other activities. Our
relationship with God also needs refreshment and renewal
to keep it strong and healthy. Time away from the daily
grind helps us to keep our perspective and remember values in the relationship that may get covered over with
too much work, fatigue, and distraction.

Even if by some chance your first experience with
retreats is disappointing, don't give up! Instead, try to take
to heart the practical advice of one young man who,
despite his active schedule, finds time to participate and
even plan weekend retreats with his church group. "Don't
write off all retreats if you don't like the first one you
attend or if it didn't seem to benefit you in some way.
There are so many kinds that no matter what it is that
you disliked about the first experience, another type of
retreat will meet your particular needs."

A good plan, if you have never made a retreat before, is to take things gently and dip your toe in the water before you take the plunge. If you are feeling apprehensive about making a retreat over several days, you are not alone! Because so many people are now looking for opportunities to make a retreat, the options available to you are increasing all the time. Some of the most popular types appear in this book, to help you feel your way and discover in a nonthreatening way just what might be helpful to you—and what will not.

The next two chapters explore in greater depth the kinds of retreats, both residential and nonresidential, that are available to those who are searching for spiritual refreshment and growth.

what is a
residential retreat?

WHETHER YOU CAN ONLY SPARE a day or two or are able to go into seclusion for weeks at a time, finding "oasis time" in retreat is an important part of the spiritual life. You need not break the bank or demolish family harmony to find it.

A retreat provides a prayerful environment where many people congregate to focus on some aspect of their journey with, and growth in, God. It is this focus, perhaps, that makes the distinction between a "spiritual holiday" and a genuine retreat. On a vacation, the focus is quite legitimately on the vacationer. On a retreat, the focus is on God, as retreatants seek to discern more deeply where God is active in their lives.

Below is an overview of some common types of residential retreats. Although these general descriptions will serve to guide you toward one option or another, every retreat house is unique. It is always best to contact directly the retreat house you have in mind to determine whether it is the right fit for you. If you are unable to get away from home, however, or if a residential retreat doesn't seem like the best option for you right now, you will find other possibilities discussed in chapter 3.

Many people making their first residential retreat choose a theme retreat as a taster experience. If, on the other hand, you wish to explore your spiritual journey more individually, you may opt for an individually given (or guided) retreat, as a theme retreat will not normally provide one-on-one guidance.

The nature of the relationship between retreatant and retreat guide will be covered more fully in chapter 4. For the present, let us simply say that having a guide feels like having a friend around. There is no compulsion to talk to your guide every day, although he or she will be available to you if you do wish to talk. On a guided retreat, your guide will not intrude into your space but will be there if you need or want to share with him or her.

THEME RETREATS

Theme retreats often span several days and are probably the most common form of retreat available.

A theme retreat may focus on almost any topic, from finding God's will for your life to studying a particular approach to spirituality. You will likely choose a particular retreat because the theme interests you, and you will be approaching the retreat in the hope of deepening your insights on the topic concerned. This topic will become the focus of your prayer during the time of the retreat.

The experience of a theme retreat is in some ways less intense than that of an individually given retreat. Though there may be periods of silence, these will be interwoven with periods of listening to the speaker or retreat leader, possibly sharing reflections with a small group of fellow retreatants, and meeting together in open forum to raise questions or make comments.

A theme retreat can last anywhere from a day to ten days or more, but the average duration lies around four or five days. If the retreat is offered in a retreat house, the cost is equivalent to that of an individually given retreat, amounting to the cost of accommodation and full board (if applicable) and the fee charged by the speaker. At current rates (2002), you would need to budget from $60 to $100 per twenty-four-hour period for a retreat including full board, and rather less if you are arranging for your own meals or if the retreat is held at a church or other day facility. The retreat house will give you full details of cost on request, and in many cases early booking is advisable.

Theme retreats vary enormously in terms of structure. However, a typical day will include time to engage in the topic or activity being explored; time alone to reflect, recreate, or simply rest and enjoy the peace; and time to be together socially with the other participants. In some cases, there will be opportunities to speak privately with the retreat leader(s)—if this is important to you it is worth checking in advance to make sure that it will be possible. Here is one example of a typical day on a theme retreat:

Between 7:30 and 9:00 A.M.	*Breakfast*
Until 10:00 A.M.	*Free time*
10:00 to 11:00 A.M.	*Presentation by the retreat guide*
11:00 A.M. to 12:00 noon	*Time for individual prayer and reflection*
12:00 to 12:45 P.M.	*Daily Eucharist*
1:00 to 2:00 P.M.	*Lunch*
2:00 to 3:00 P.M.	*Presentation by the retreat guide*
3:00 to 4:00 P.M.	*Time for individual prayer and reflection*
4:00 to 6:00 P.M.	*Free time*
6:00 to 7:00 P.M.	*Dinner*
7:00 to 8:00 P.M.	*Free time*
8:00 to 9:00 P.M.	*Group sharing or open forum*
9:00 to 9:30 P.M.	*Shared evening prayer*

Generally speaking, there is less free time on a theme retreat than there is on an individually guided retreat. And yet, this plan is also very flexible. Sometimes the retreat leader will give only one presentation, sometimes two or even three. There may well be an evening presentation, leaving the entire afternoon free. In some cases the time between presentations will be a time of strict silence, sometimes not.

Usually, theme retreats that are based around a common interest or activity do not assume any previous knowledge or level of ability. Anyone is welcome. Many people who would say, for example, that they cannot draw or cannot write, nevertheless greatly enjoy the opportunity to exercise their creativity when there is no demand to "achieve" anything. Such activities can be powerful means of exploring what is going on in one's own hidden depths.

As an example, here is one woman's story of spiritual discovery:

It was a great relief when our artist retreat leader said we had to come with an empty mind. My mind was completely empty—I was not artsy, and I had no craft skills. I was not sure why I was there to pray the passion and cross of Jesus in paint, clay, sculptural relief, and mixed media.

"Let's start by making a cross out of newspaper," said our leader. I couldn't believe my response. I did not want to make a cross. I could not make a cross, and I felt like a stubborn child. I needed to reflect on this.

Crosses were painful, destructive, agonizing experiences, not to be trivialized. I couldn't make a cross of newspaper. I had come to the retreat to know God more, so I thought a ladder to climb up to him might be more appropriate. So I made a paper ladder. But no, that was not right. God was a presence within me, not up there, so with some force and satisfaction, I crunched the ladder into a ball.

Then I found myself adding layers of newspaper and colored paper around this ball. Were these the layers of myself, which had to be removed in order to know more of this mystery called God? I knew there were parts of me that sometimes held me back from reaching out to others. I wanted to cross this gulf and give myself freely.

I soon had a crumpled paper ball a little smaller than a soccer ball. It needed to be held together, so I stuck on two lengths of white tape only to see, to my surprise, that I had made a cross. I still did not want a cross, so I placed two more pieces of tape and felt that the ball/me was now held together in the security of love.

I reflected on the paper ball overnight. I thought of the time of my own crucifixion—a time of anguish with a nightmare quality to it. This had lasted a long time, yet my faith in a positive outcome was never in doubt, and in the end I was strengthened in my certainty of God's presence in all that happens to us. But it did not feel like that at the time!

So now I wished that I had placed a cross at the center of my ball.

The next morning I talked to our artist prayer companion, and we agreed to open the ball to see what was inside and to place a cross there. It was difficult to cut through the screwed up paper, but I managed it, and I made a little wooden cross and covered it in gold paper. The cross was an essential part of me; it had given me the experience of the compassion and glory of love. . . .

[Later,] I had time for quiet reflection in the chapel, holding my crumpled ball with the golden cross secure in the middle. Then the true nature of crucifixion—Jesus' and mine—came to me. It was a falling apart, a disintegration, a losing of all that had meaning, all security. Could I allow my own ball creation to remain fragile and vulnerable? After more reflection, I knew that the only honest thing to do was to leave it without support, to accept the possibility of its fragmentation. Disintegration and fragmentation *were words and experiences to be avoided, but I was not distressed. I knew that through these experiences it was possible to be held together and renewed. By what? That is the Mystery!*

The opportunity to share something of this exploration with others who are on the same wavelength is one of the great benefits of this type of retreat and can be a powerful catalyst for personal growth. Sometimes life-long friendships are formed during these periods.

Depending upon your needs, there are a couple of alternatives to a theme retreat that might work for you.

Retreat weekends

A shorter form of the theme retreat, sometimes called a theme retreat weekend, offers retreatants the opportunity to go away from Friday evening to Sunday afternoon, enjoying two nights and two days in a retreat center, with full board. Or it may be held in a church or other facility and offer only snacks or one simple meal. However, the weekends themselves tend to fall into three main categories:

• Weekends to focus on a particular topic (such as Celtic or Orthodox spirituality), a particular aspect of practical spirituality (such as finding God's will), or a particular season in the Church calendar (such as a Lenten retreat).

• Weekends for a particular group of people to explore their own needs and feelings in a safe environment. Examples include weekends for the bereaved, for singles, or for married couples. Some centers also offer weekends especially for those with special needs, such as a weekend for the deaf conducted in sign language.

• Weekends to pursue a particular activity with like-minded people. These include weekends for painting, embroidery, calligraphy, circle dancing, and many more. Of course these activities can also be pursued in a prayerful setting over a longer period. "Walking retreats" are also becoming increasingly popular, encouraging participants to enjoy the countryside (or indeed the cityscape) creatively and prayerfully.

Do-it-yourself weekends

If you are involved with any kind of faith-sharing group or spirituality network, you will almost certainly want to arrange quiet days or weekends for your group. Many retreat centers will welcome your use of their facilities while allowing you to arrange your own time in your own way. Usually the retreat center will ask for only a modest donation to cover costs. They will almost always be able to offer beverages and a place for you to enjoy a sack lunch. They may also offer soup and sandwiches or a full lunch by arrangement. Some practical guidelines for planning a group retreat are offered at the end of this chapter. See page 51.

If you are looking for two days of space and silence with no instruction or interaction with other retreatants, you might prefer to find a monastic center, many of which welcome weekend or short-term visitors to enjoy their hospitality and join in their community prayer. A weekend such as this would be unstructured apart from the daily offices, and you would be free to shape it to your own needs entirely. There would almost certainly be someone available to listen if you wished to talk one-on-one.

SUSTAINED SILENT RETREATS

I once met someone on a quiet day in a retreat center who told me that this was the first time in over twenty years that she had been able to spend as much as a single hour alone in silence. All those years she had been surrounded by her husband, children, or work colleagues. The quiet day gave her space to just stand still and observe something of the shape and focus of her life.

Today, perhaps more than ever before, many people long for such space, and a surprising number of them rarely, if ever, manage to get it. You might like to reflect for a moment on what these words mean to you: *space, solitude, silence.* If there is a voice in your depths crying out for just those things, then you will probably want to consider making a sustained retreat (perhaps a week or longer) in a center or monastic house somewhere far away from home and work.

If this is your desire, there are a number of possibilities available to you. You may choose an individually guided retreat. You might also opt for a period of retreat in a religious house or retreat center with no personal guidance. Or you may decide to go on a period of retreat alone, wherever you feel drawn to be. Which retreat option you choose will depend to a large degree upon what you want to get out of the experience.

Individually given retreats (IGRs)

The words "individually given," or "individually guided," might strike fear into the heart of a would-be retreat maker. This reaction may be even more intense if you hear these terms reduced to their initials and are left wondering what on earth you are getting yourself into if you take on an IGR.

Simply put, an individually given retreat is a period of retreat usually (though not necessarily) conducted in silence, in which you will have an individual companion who will accompany you in prayer in a special way through the days of your retreat. This person will also be available by appointment for regular, personal, one-on-one meetings. This companion will be a person of prayer and of empathy who will be looking forward to making the retreat journey with you. He or she will appreciate what a genuine privilege it is to be invited to share in another person's sacred story. Chapter 4 will provide more information on the nature of this companion and his or her role in the retreat.

Many people about to go on retreat find themselves wondering what a typical day in an individually given retreat will be like. While every retreat house has its own routine and no two retreats are the same, it may be helpful to give a couple of examples of how a day might run on retreat. Please bear in mind that this is only an example and that no fixed routine will be imposed on you. You are a free citizen and may choose to miss meals, to go off for an outing, or to do whatever you wish with your time.

A typical day on an individually given retreat might look something like this:

Between 7:30 and 9:00 A.M.	*Breakfast*
9:00 A.M. to 12:00 noon	*Your own time*
12:00 to 12:45 P.M.	*Daily Eucharist*
1:00 to 2:00 P.M.	*Lunch*
2:00 to 5:30 P.M.	*Your own time*
5:30 to 6:30 P.M.	*Dinner*
6:30 to 8:00 P.M.	*Your own time*
8:00 to 8:30 P.M.	*Shared evening prayer*

Your meeting with your guide would be arranged during one of the periods of free time. For more about this, see chapter 4.

As you can see, there is considerable time for you to do as you wish. Some of this time will certainly be spent in prayer and reflection, but it is also wise to allow some time for rest and relaxation, and perhaps for taking a walk.

First-time residential retreats

Your first time making a retreat can be something of a culture shock, especially if you are used to a noisy and demanding environment or workplace. Many retreat centers now offer retreats specially tailored for those who have never made a retreat before. While a standard residential retreat tends to last for a week or more, a first-time retreat will usually be shorter, perhaps just a few days or a weekend.

If the retreat is basically a silent one, you will probably find the silence to be less absolute in a first-time retreat. There may be more opportunities for verbal interaction with the retreat leaders or even with the other participants. You will be able to experience the deep silence of a retreat, but possibly for only a few hours at a time. The idea is to offer retreatants a taste of the experience of an individually given retreat in a silent or near-silent situation, with the focus on prayer and reflection.

Those who offer first-time retreats understand the anxieties many people feel prior to their first retreat experience. They will often offer help in dealing with these matters. For example, in a guided retreat your guide may suggest ways of structuring the day so as to reach a good balance of rest, prayer, and recreation. Many first-time retreats will also suggest approaches to personal prayer that you may not have tried before. Guidance may also be offered on using art or clay to help you in your prayer, and you may have the opportunity to share your experience with a small group of other retreatants if you so wish.

Often a first-time retreat will include more time to be together with the others who are making the retreat than would normally be the case. The silence will usually be broken up by periods of meeting together to reflect on various aspects of the process of making the retreat. There may be opportunities for sharing your questions, your feelings, or your general experience of the retreat with the rest of the group, though there should never be any pressure to do so.

If interested, call your local retreat centers and ask if they offer retreats especially for the first-timer. If the center you call doesn't offer this program, the person you speak with may still be able to recommend one that does. If you locate a retreat that looks good to you and you would like to find out more about it, don't hesitate to phone that retreat center and ask. They are there to help you, and they will welcome your inquiry.

Quiet days

If you are unsure about committing yourself to a longer retreat, why not try a "quiet day"? Many retreat centers offer quiet days as a regular feature of their programs. Some parishes also offer them from time to time. A quiet day can take any form, but it will always offer you a space of reflective calm and usually also some kind of input to help you find inner stillness and to deepen your spiritual life in some way.

Quiet days fall into several categories:

• Days centered on a particular theme, often with a short talk or series of talks given by a speaker or retreat leader. A theme day such as this might begin with a short time of quiet to help participants settle in. A talk or presentation may follow, with time afterward for private reflection, group sharing, or an open forum in which questions and comments can be raised.

• Days simply offering a quiet place, with no input or at most a period of led prayer. There may also be an opportunity to speak with someone one-on-one if you wish.

• Days centered on a particular activity. A day of this nature might include some instruction on the spiritual dimension or application of the activity concerned. It will certainly include plenty of opportunity to meet with others who enjoy the same activity.

• So-called taster days that allow you to try out new approaches to prayer, for example. These are an excellent introduction to personal prayer and may be a good place to begin your explorations if you are thinking of making a retreat for the first time.

A quiet day typically lasts from about 10:00 A.M. to 4:00 P.M. The cost can vary enormously, from as little as $10 to $50 or more. This will depend upon what is being included (some quiet days include morning coffee, lunch, and afternoon refreshments) and on the cost of renting the location and covering the expenses of any presenters. If lunch is not included, you may be expected to bring your own sack lunch or to contribute a dish to a potluck.

These days will normally be led by someone experienced in retreat giving who will share some thoughts on an aspect of the inner journey or the practice of prayer and reflection. The leader may also make him- or herself available to anyone who would like to talk privately. The purpose of this input is not to offer a course of instruction, but to suggest some ways of focusing your thoughts and going deeper into the stillness where you are touching the ground of your being and the dwelling place of God within you. If the input isn't helpful to you personally, then leave it aside and follow the promptings of your own heart. Nothing is compulsory during a day of retreat like this.

The main part of the day will offer time simply to be still, to pray, to reflect, to ponder, to *be*. Usually there will be ample space for people to spread out through the house and find a congenial spot to be alone and at peace. You can use the time in any way you choose, provided that you allow others their space and their silence. The day may well include a period of shared prayer or worship and possibly a more formal service, perhaps with communion. Again, attendance is voluntary.

It should also be noted that many centers that are used for quiet days are very welcoming of people who wish merely to drop in for some quiet, perhaps just for a short while, and then go on their way. If you are looking for an oasis of calm, you will find it in such a center, and no one will bother you or ask what you are up to. However, if you want to talk to someone, this is usually possible on request. "Droppers in" are usually welcome to join in any of the prayer or worship that may be going on in the center at the time.

Finally, some churches or organizations hold local or national "days of prayer" from time to time. They may mark the anniversary of a significant event or focus on prayer support for some particular issue or concern. Such events are often advertised beyond the normal boundaries of a particular parish or office and welcome people who are not normally associated with the sponsoring organization.

Ongoing spiritual companionship

If the idea of making a structured retreat and following a specific program does not appeal to you, but you are look-ing for individual spiritual companionship or soul friend-ship, you should be able to find someone in your area who would welcome a chance to share the journey with you and who is experienced in accompanying others in prayer and spiritual exploration. This topic will be addressed more fully in chapter 4. Alternatively, a national organization such as Christian Life Community (see appendix 1 at the back of the book) will be able to give you the name of a local contact person who will in turn get in touch with a network of fellow pilgrims. You are then quite free to follow up on any suggested contacts.

Retreats on the streets

For many people, especially those who are active in the causes of justice and peace, the idea of a quiet day "away from it all" can sound escapist (although I hope that this book will convince you that this is not the case). A retreat can be a very active undertaking and a way of making a radical identification with the marginalized people in our communities.

In some towns it is possible to make a retreat on the streets. This involves a day of walking the streets and seeking to engage the real needs and feelings of those who are living there not by choice, but of necessity.

This kind of retreat can take many forms. A typical day might begin with shared prayer and ecumenical worship and a simple shared breakfast, after which the participants go off into the city with only a couple of dollars to fend for themselves. The retreatants become more deeply aware of how it feels to be on the streets with less than the cost of a simple meal in their pockets. They are free to shape the day in their own way, but may well take the opportunity to talk with those they meet who are homeless, unemployed, disturbed, or addicted. While this offers only a glimpse of the stark reality of street life, it is nevertheless a deeply moving and challenging experience for those who undertake it.

The day often ends with a chance to gather again with the other participants and share the insights and feelings of the day. This often leads to new initiatives for relieving the suffering that has been witnessed.

EXTENDED RETREATS

Perhaps, like me, you look back over major life decisions you have made in the past and wonder, "What was I thinking of when I chose that course?" Hindsight often makes us wish that we had known then what we know now, saving us a great deal of heartache and disappointment.

Well, what we do know now is that our decisions are better made with God. One way to approach a major life choice in the future might be to reflect deeply in a time of retreat upon the implications of the choice. Of course, a retreat will not grant us guarantees as to how our choices are going to work out in practice. It can, however, give us the time and the space to seriously discern what we most deeply want and which direction our inner wisdom will seek out.

This kind of discernment lies at the heart of what is sometimes called the long retreat (or the thirty- or forty-day retreat). A sustained time of retreat may help you to face a big question in your life, perhaps about your future course of work, your commitment to a cause, the decision to marry or to have a family, or, less happily, to end a destructive relationship or leave an exploitative work situation.

The details of the Spiritual Exercises of St. Ignatius of Loyola, which forms the basis of most extended retreats, will be fully addressed in chapter 8. However, please note that if you apply to make the full Exercises in the seclusion of a retreat center, you may find that the organizers will ask for references and reserve the right to reject your application. The process is demanding physically, emotionally, and spiritually, and the retreat center needs to have some assurance that you will be able to cope with the demands of such intensive prayer within an environment of near-total silence. It would in any case be unwise to enter into the process of the full Exercises without having first made a few shorter silent, individually given retreats and without having had the experience of ongoing spiritual direction (or soul friendship) in daily life.

This type of experience can also be somewhat costly. At the time of this publication (2002), room and board at a retreat center for thirty to thirty-six days would run from $60 to $100 per twenty-four-hour period, a bit less if you arrange for your own meals.

That said, making the full Exercises of St. Ignatius can be a life-changing and deeply rewarding experience. The Exercises are structured in a way that encourages the retreatant to reflect on the implications of the choice in question, to make a decision, and to seek to confirm this decision through prayer. The retreatant will usually be accompanied by an experienced retreat director who is familiar with the dynamics of the Exercises and will be able to act as a colistener to the promptings and movements arising in your heart from the days and weeks of prayer.

If a structured set of Exercises is not for you, however, there are other ways of taking significant time out in seclusion and silence, with or without a personal guide. Long retreats will follow a pattern similar to that of any individually given retreat. They will, however, normally be preceded by a few days of acclimatization before the silence begins to give you an opportunity to reflect on your journey so far and what you are hoping for from the retreat, and perhaps to meet other people who will be making the retreat at the same time and place.

During most extended retreats, there will normally be three or four rest days when the silence may be lifted and you will be free to relax in your own way. For some people, these days can feel like an intrusion into the silence; for others they are an essential loosening of the intensity of the experience. Of course, if you don't want to break your silence, there is no obligation to do so.

There will frequently be a few days after the silence ends to review the experience for yourself, or with others if you wish. These final few days are an important buffer zone between the silence of seclusion and the hustle and bustle of the daily activities to which you will be returning. They help to reduce the shock of returning to your everyday life.

CHOOSING A RETREAT CENTER

Now that you have determined which kind of retreat you would like to make, it is time to decide which retreat center will best suit you. Appendix 1 at the end of this book offers some possibilities, and there are many beautiful centers that you can find on the Internet or through your church. There is often quite a range of retreat centers to choose from in a given area.

If you are thinking of making a residential retreat, how do you decide where to go? It is best to begin by answering some basic questions regarding your needs and expectations. Here are some points to consider:

Will meals be provided?

Your budget may decide this question for you. For obvious reasons, retreats in which you provide your own meals are generally less expensive than full-board accommodations. Both have their advantages. In a self-catering retreat, you have greater control over your own time. On the other hand, providing yourself with meals is a task that you might like to be free of for a while. Self-catering retreats often take place in small cottages or in annexes to larger retreat houses, thus intensifying the sense of isolation. This may be exactly what you want, or it may become oppressive—it depends a great deal on your own personality and on how comfortable you are in your own company.

Simplicity or luxury?

Again, this will often be a matter of cost as well as of personal preference. Most retreat houses offer good, wholesome food, ranging from "simple" to "very satisfying." A retreat house is not a luxury liner, and most people would not wish it to be so. In most centers there are tea- and coffee-making facilities available throughout the day and night, often in kitchenettes close to the retreatants' bedrooms. Some of the larger houses are upgrading their accommodations to provide such amenities in each room. If you are looking for comfort and privacy and are prepared to pay for it, you may want to restrict your search to these larger houses. On the other hand, often the *atmosphere* of a retreat house is more important to retreatants than the size or quality of their bedrooms. If you prefer more basic accommodations, a center that offers a welcoming sense of warmth and a certain character that differentiates it from a boarding school will help you feel at home.

The gardens and surrounding landscape can also be an important factor in choosing a retreat center. Most houses have gardens that are conducive to quiet reflection, and some are set in a beautiful landscape among hills or by the seashore. Look out for this if it is important to you to be able to go for walks straight from the retreat house door without negotiating roads or having to drive.

Silent or not-so-silent?

Most individually given residential retreats are advertised as being conducted in silence. However, there are degrees of silence, and some retreat houses safeguard the silence better than others. This is not the kind of information you will find in promotional books or leaflets. If it is important to you that the silence be truly respected throughout your retreat, you might do well to speak with someone who has experience with different retreat houses.

Personal reactions to silence vary widely. Some people find it oppressive and will look for a more gregarious experience the next time around. For others, the silence becomes a haven that they seek out year after year.

As a general principle, you will find that the silence is more absolute in retreat houses that are devoted solely to the giving of silent retreats. If there are other events, such as courses, going on at the same time, the silence will inevitably be compromised a little, though people who are not in retreat will normally be asked to respect the quiet of those who are. In the best retreat houses, you can depend on an atmosphere of silence even when retreats and courses are running concurrently, to the extent that meals will be offered at different times to those in retreat.

Spontaneous or planned?

Whether you need to book ahead depends a great deal on where you want to go and when. Many retreat houses, especially the better-known ones, can be booked up to a year or more in advance, especially during school holiday periods. Similarly, many smaller retreat centers, with perhaps just a few bedrooms, also fill up quickly.

If a particular theme retreat attracts you, it is wise to make up your mind quickly and call the retreat center to inquire about reserving a place. Usually a center will accept a phone booking if it is followed up within the next few days with a written confirmation and a deposit. Some retreat centers have Web sites that will indicate the current availability of retreat spaces—but don't rely too heavily on these. It is usually better to check personally by phone or by letter. If you do make a written inquiry, be sure to enclose a stamped, self-addressed envelope for the reply.

Theme retreats tend to be advertised in a retreat center's publicity brochures, which are usually issued once or twice a year. Retreats in daily life are usually only advertised locally, around the center where they are being held (parish, school, college, etc.). Because of the nature of a daily-life retreat (see chapter 3), it is not so crucial to book ahead; extra prayer companions/prayer guides are welcomed to join the retreat. Such a retreat allows for a more flexible situation; it is conducted on a commuting rather than a residential basis, and boarding space is not an issue.

If you have set your heart on making an individually given retreat in a particular retreat center, contact the center as soon as you are able to give definite dates. Many people are disappointed every year because they have waited too long to make arrangements to join the retreat of their choice. Most retreat centers, however, also hold waiting lists. Because of the long lead time between booking and actually making the retreat, there is a reasonable chance of being offered a place if you are near the top of the waiting list.

What if I can't afford to go on retreat?

Many retreat centers offer price reductions for students or for those with low incomes or on welfare. Many also have scholarship funds available to help people who would not otherwise have the financial means to make a retreat. This money has been given over the years by people who wanted to help others to make a retreat.

If you need financial help, do not hesitate to explain your situation to the director or administrator of the retreat. If such funds are available at a particular retreat house, they are there to be used. Your request for help will not affect your chance of being offered a retreat space. If there is help available, your request will be considered, and you will be given a straightforward answer. As was noted at the beginning of the chapter, there is no need to "break the bank" in order to meet with God.

THE COST OF RETREATS

There is, of course, no such thing as a typical retreat, and it follows that any indication of likely cost is merely a very broad guideline. The range of retreat costs starts at almost nothing and spirals up into thousands of dollars. The cost of a retreat depends a great deal on whether or not those offering the retreat are doing so as their only means of making a living. When this is the case, we must expect realistic (but not profit-making) charges for the services being offered.

Low-cost retreats

The lowest-cost retreats are retreats in daily life (see chapter 3), organized and accompanied by a volunteer prayer companion/prayer guide. You can expect to be asked for only a nominal contribution toward the expenses of the prayer companions and the cost of renting the venue, if applicable. At current (2002) rates, this might be as low as $10.00 per person for a week of guided prayer that is being offered on a local basis. If the prayer companions are traveling from far away, this cost might increase proportionately. Using public facilities (other than a church hall) for the opening, closing, and one-on-one meetings will also add to the cost. If you decide to use a church hall, remember that it may be difficult to get the space you need at certain times of the year.

Some centers offer a wonderful range of quiet days, days of reflection, or drop-in days on a donation basis. This means that you will be asked to make a donation within your own means toward the cost of the day. Sometimes a suggested level of donation will be mentioned. A donation, however, is what it says it is. No one will be checking up on what each person has offered. The whole idea is to make access to such days as wide-ranging as possible so that no one is excluded because they can't afford it.

Higher-cost retreats

Obviously, as soon as accommodations and meals are required, the cost of a retreat goes up. We all know what food, heating, lighting, insurance, and all the other costs of running a household amount to today, and every retreat center carries these costs as well as the costs of cleaning and household maintenance, often in buildings that are beautiful, old, large, full of atmosphere, and exceedingly expensive to maintain.

On a residential retreat, you need to budget for what you would normally expect to pay for bed, breakfast, lunch, and evening meals anywhere else. What is actually offered for this price is usually, however, a lot more than you would find in normal vacation lodgings. In an individually given retreat, for example, it includes daily sessions with the retreat guide, the daily liturgies, and the invitation to be not so much a guest as a member of the family for the duration of your stay. Again, most retreat centers will invite a suggested offering (though this should not be regarded as optional). At current (2002) prices, this might range from $60 to $100 for each twenty-four-hour period.

Once you have budgeted for the retreat itself, however, there is virtually no other cost except that of getting there and back. While you are there you will need nothing else—unless, of course, you are a bookworm, as most retreat centers run very tempting bookstores!

Some one-day events can be more costly than others. If, for example, a speaker must travel from some distance away, or more expensive quarters are needed, a single day of reflection can sometimes cost $45.00 or more, though sometimes discounts are available to those with low incomes.

THEME RETREATS FOR PREEXISTING GROUPS

It often happens that a number of people who already know each other well choose to make a retreat together as a discrete group. They may be from the same church or neighborhood, or from an existing prayer group or group of colleagues engaged in the same kind of work. By its nature, such a retreat will normally be a theme retreat, focusing on some aspect of the common life and quest of the people in the group. The group will plan for the retreat, taking into account the various hopes and expectations of all concerned, just as a family might plan a vacation together. Indeed, some retreats like this are called "church getaways," but they have a strong spiritual focus and can therefore truly be regarded as retreats.

Such a period of time away together can be enormously strengthening and enriching to the people who make it. A bonding is possible on retreat that goes beyond the normal interactions of group or parish life. Living together in community and exploring together some aspect of their journey of faith creates an opportunity for a new surge of growth and can be a catalyst for new beginnings in the wider community from which the group is drawn.

The form of such a group retreat will normally follow the same broad pattern as that described for theme retreats in general. There will be time for shared worship and prayer, for some kind of teaching or focus sessions, perhaps led by an outside facilitator, and for shared leisure and social time.

If you are planning a group retreat of this nature, you might like to give some thought to the following considerations:

• *How many people are interested in making the retreat?* You will need to have a fairly definite idea of numbers before booking the venue, and this implies the need for a degree of commitment by the participants. It will enable you to decide the cost per head, the necessary deposit, and the extent of the accommodations required.

• *Who is the retreat for?* Is it intended to offer a retreat, for example, to a group of people who have the same general expectations (such as a prayer group), or is this to be open to the members of a wider group, such as a parish community? In the latter case, how are you going to provide for the needs of all age groups? If the retreat is to be accessible to young families, for example, there will need to be reliable child care available, and good leadership for children's and young people's activities as well as the material for the adult sessions. Bear in mind that parents will appreciate some time to make something of a retreat themselves, free of the responsibility for their children, if only for an hour at a time, so plan to have some activities for the younger members of the group that are led by someone other than their parents. If child care is to be provided for babies and toddlers, this too needs careful prearranging. Sometimes babysitters are brought along, and parents of the very small may be willing to arrange a rotation for nursery duty.

• *What kind of focus is required?* Take care to choose a theme for the reflection sessions that will speak to all present. For a prayer group or a group of colleagues working in the same environment, this will be relatively easy. For a parish group ranging in age from newborn to centenarian and across all ability ranges, it will be a much more challenging task to find the right focus and to find a speaker who will be sensitive to the diversity of the group. But the results can be well worth the effort.

• *What will the program be?* You will need to strike a kind of balance between shared worship, study or reflection sessions, and leisure time. Establish a consensus on this by consulting those who hope to make the retreat and drawing up a plan well ahead of time. If the group includes all ages, a common pattern is to leave every afternoon free for people to enjoy as they wish, and it may be helpful to arrange some entertainment on at least one of the evenings. This may be as simple as showing a video, or it may be an opportunity for the parish to put on its own show. A special quality of togetherness is fostered when everyone in a diverse group can truly enjoy such an occasion.

• *How will we get the word out?* If you choose to include others outside your immediate group in the event, be creative in generating word of mouth among those who might be interested. Posters, notices in church bulletins, e-mail messages, and (most importantly) personal invitations will help.

• *How can we continue to benefit from the retreat after it ends?* Consider making an audio recording of the main events and sessions of the retreat, including the shared worship, for the benefit of those who were unable to attend and as an aid to ongoing reflections for those who were there.

• *If possible, visit the site beforehand.* It is a good idea for a member of the group to visit the center beforehand to check the parking arrangements and the accommodations, and to establish rapport with the center leaders.

Without a doubt, arranging a group retreat is hard work, especially if the retreatants come in all ages, but the fruits will not disappoint you. Again and again, people return to their groups or parishes from group retreats with new energy and sharpened vision and enthusiasm that spreads out in ripples beyond the boundaries of the group itself. The fruit of these retreats yields seed for fresh growth in the wider community.

As a general rule, aim to keep the costs within the range of the least privileged members of the community. Many retreat houses and Christian hotels are happy to welcome groups who are working within a strict budget and will do all they can to keep costs to a minimum. Expenditure can also be eased by asking participants to share cars for the journey to and from the retreat location, and by planning to make the retreat in off-peak times of the year. Reduce costs further by holding the retreat at a central location, such as a parish hall (although this will mean more work for the individuals planning the retreat).

Days of retreat may be organized by a church group or service organization in order to minister to the needs of a

particular segment of the parish. Before you get too far
into the planning of this event, check with your church
administrator to see if funds are available from the church
budget to assist you and to help defray the cost for those
who plan to attend.

   If no such funds are available, there are a number of
ways to keep the cost at a minimum:

• Find someone in the parish who would be willing to
volunteer his or her services as a speaker. Don't forget to
send a thank-you note, perhaps with a small token of
thanks, after the event is over.

• Ask members of the planning group to contribute items
for a simple potluck breakfast or morning break, to keep
food costs to a minimum.

• Consider hiring a teenager (who may be willing to
work in exchange for confirmation "service points") to
provide child care for those attending the retreat. A suitable area will need to be set up ahead of time for this
purpose.

• Minimize the use of handouts and costly decorations.
Elaborate programs and brochures can be distracting,
although it may be helpful to have any song lyrics or
prayers printed on a transparency and displayed with an
overhead projector. A few simple cuttings from the garden are all you need to spruce up the service table.

can i still
make a retreat
if i can't get away?

IN A CULTURE that values freedom so highly, it is quite amazing how many of us are, in effect, prisoners of our personal circumstances. Sometimes this sense of being trapped in our own little world is a mere inconvenience. Sometimes it feels like a dead weight upon our lives.

For example, single parents with young children rarely have time to themselves. "Going out" means taking the children to school or wheeling them around in a grocery cart. They might occasionally spend an hour with a friend over coffee, chatting while they supervise the little ones. Adult companionship and time "just to be" are rare luxuries.

There are many other circumstances whereby people must endure virtual house arrest. The following are a few examples:

• People who are caring for sick or elderly relatives.

• People who are sick or convalescing and are unable to go out independently.

• People who, for whatever reason, are afraid to venture out alone.

• People who are trying to grow spiritually but are faced with resistance or even outright opposition from a partner or immediate family member.

The popularity of retreats has grown tremendously in recent years. Many more people have heard of the possibility of making a retreat, and by the same token, many people have felt this to be an impossible dream for one or more of the reasons mentioned above. Necessity has once again proved to be the mother of invention, however, and much thought has been given to the challenge of opening up the retreat experience to those many people who, for personal or financial reasons, cannot leave home for any length of time.

RETREAT OPTIONS

There are a number of possibilities for those who cannot get away from their immediate circumstances for long periods of time.

Retreats in daily life

A retreat in daily life is an opportunity to set aside a special time—perhaps a week or even several weeks—during which you give time to prayer each day and meet with an experienced companion, commonly called a prayer companion or a prayer guide. You might meet with this companion either daily for about half an hour (in a one-week intensive retreat) or once or twice a week during a longer retreat. This type of retreat, often called a week (or weeks) of guided prayer, offers many of the benefits of a residential retreat without leaving one's normal day-to-day commitments.

Deborah, a working mother who happens to be a lawyer, reported that she was delighted with the results of her first daily-life retreat.

The retreat was structured over a six-week period. It commenced with an introductory meeting, which was attended by all pilgrims and prayer guides. The closing evening was also attended by all pilgrims and prayer guides and provided an opportunity to share our retreat experiences, both positive and negative, and to pray together. In the intervening weeks arrangements were made between the pilgrim and prayer guide to meet each week for about half an hour, at a time and place convenient to both. I met my prayer guide each Friday at 8:15 A.M. in Birmingham Cathedral, and on each occasion we found a quiet corner to talk and pray without disturbing others or being disturbed, except on our last meeting, when the organist had an early practice!

During the first week I prayed imaginatively from Scripture and was amazed at the way God spoke to me directly about every part of my life—home, work, and church. In the following weeks I prayed meditatively from Scripture, and again God spoke to me in the stillness about all aspects of my life and matters that were currently troubling me as well as certain traumatic events in the past.

I was helped enormously by my prayer guide, who was a wise, discerning, godly woman with the gift of listening. At our weekly meetings to discuss my prayer journey she led me to passages of Scripture to pray over—sometimes a short psalm, sometimes a longer passage—to enable me to continue my journey. She simply listened and only offered advice when I asked for it. The passages of Scripture she suggested were always relevant and helpful. I felt that the way she listened and gently suggested the next step reflected the gentle and loving way God was leading me in my prayer journey.

I was only able to devote about ten minutes each day to prayer yet God honored that commitment, and I was amazed how God spoke during these short periods of stillness and quiet.

A retreat in daily life is a variation of the individually given retreat, in that you will have a personal companion to accompany you through the period of the retreat. The most commonly used models for this kind of retreat are the week of guided prayer and the extended retreat in daily life. The week of guided prayer, which lasts for five, six, or seven consecutive days, entails a daily meeting with your prayer companion or prayer guide. The extended retreat in daily life, which is spread over four, five, or six weeks, or even longer, usually entails a weekly meeting with the companion.

Both ways of offering a daily-life retreat begin with a welcome meeting for all those making the retreat, and for their prayer companions. Usually this meeting will include some time for reflection, an explanation of how the retreat will proceed, and an opportunity to meet your companion and arrange the times you will meet during the retreat. A similar gathering will happen at the end of the retreat, when the whole group will come together again to share in reflection, to talk about their experiences, and perhaps to have a small celebration together. All that is asked of you in making a daily-life retreat is

• To commit yourself to a time of prayer each day during the retreat. Some guides may suggest a minimum period of about ten to fifteen minutes, and they will be glad to help you find fruitful approaches to prayer and to reflective living.

• To commit yourself to meeting your guide promptly at the arranged time and to share with him or her anything that you feel comfortable in sharing.

The venue for a daily-life retreat might be almost anywhere. The most common location is a church hall, a rectory, presbytery, or manse, or a school or parish hall of some kind, at least for the opening and closing meetings. The one-on-one meetings with your guide may be arranged in a private home, either your own or the guide's, or in any other mutually convenient location where you will have enough privacy to speak freely.

In general, the organization and the companioning ministry in a daily-life retreat are offered on a voluntary basis. This means that the cost to you should be low, amounting only to a sum sufficient to cover the necessary expenses of the people involved, including rental space, if applicable. If you are concerned about cost, ask the organizers what your expenses will be. Understand, too, that people who have no other means of support usually charge a fee or ask for a donation when offering spiritual companionship.

Initiating a daily-life retreat. The idea of a daily-life retreat is gaining ground, and you may find that one of your local churches is offering this possibility. If not, contact a spirituality network or organization in your area and ask its organizers for information on any daily-life retreats that may be coming up. If there are none, ask for one. You may find that the network will be glad to initiate plans for a retreat.

A retreat can happen wherever two or more with the desire to make a retreat are gathered. There is no need to wait for a long line of would-be retreatants. Be persistent, if necessary, and don't take no for an answer. Think ecumenically, and if your own tradition and its local leaders seem to be unwilling or unable to offer daily-life retreats, approach the others. There is nothing in the rules of any tradition that forbids us to pray together!

Practicalities. Apart from the time set aside for prayer and the time for talking with your companion, your daily routine continues unchanged during the course of such a retreat. The cost is minimal, as these retreats are often centered in a local parish or church community, or even in a workplace or school. The only expense incurred would be the cost of travel for you and the prayer companion. In some cases, if you are housebound, the companion will be able to visit you in your own home.

In any form of daily-life retreat, your retreat companion will suggest a focus for your prayer during the time between meetings. He or she will simply *accompany* you. There will be no attempt to persuade you along paths you do not choose or to influence you in any way. You are the pilgrim, choosing for yourself how you will make the journey. The companion will simply listen and reflect back to you anything you have shared that sheds light on the way your journey is evolving.

You might first approach your local church leaders to ask whether any facilities for making a daily life retreat exist in your area. If not, you might be able to persuade them to think about arranging one. Otherwise, try making contact with representatives of one of the growing number of spirituality networks, who should be able to put you in touch with local opportunities.

Open-door retreats

The retreats sponsored by the Cenacle Sisters are a good example of how the retreat movement has changed over the years to respond to the real needs of people. Faced with the challenge of offering sacred space to people in confining situations, the Cenacle Sisters have developed their special vision of open-door retreats, which are a more structured form of retreat in daily life. These faith-sharing meetings may be done in small groups or one-on-one with a retreat companion. Such retreats offer an opportunity to explore the most important questions of your inner journey. Your companion or companions will listen to your story and help you to discern where God has been active in your life and where you feel he is leading you now.

This experience is based on the principles of St. Ignatius of Loyola, whose insights have shaped the way in which many individually given retreats are conducted. Your companion will have been specifically trained in the giving of open-door retreats and will offer you space to explore your own issues within a framework of scriptural reflections and personal prayer. An open-door retreat involves the following:

• Attendance at a two-hour session once a week for nine consecutive weeks, during which you will meet with others who are also making the retreat. You will be asked to attend all sessions and to arrive punctually unless unforeseen circumstances arise.

• A commitment to spend at least fifteen minutes each day in personal prayer and reflection.

• A willingness to share with the group something of the experience of your week's prayer.

• An agreement to be bound to absolute confidentiality with regard to everything that is shared in the group meetings.

The weekly meetings of open-door retreats are usually led by a team of two people who have made an open-door retreat themselves and have also been trained to lead such retreats. The leaders will also be making the retreat with you and will share something of their own experience of prayer and of the challenge to live a Christ-centered life. They will also be available to help individuals on a one-on-one basis, facilitate the meetings, listen sensitively to all that is shared, and encourage the whole group along its journey.

The retreat takes the general form of an opening session, which mainly offers an introduction to the process and an idea of what to expect, usually followed by seven or eight weekly meetings. During the week following this first meeting, you will probably want to reflect on whether this is a journey you want to make. If you feel that you are not able to enter into this kind of commitment at this time, or if you have doubts of any other nature, you are completely free to opt out at this point. The whole purpose of the first session is to give you time to reflect and to make a good choice as to whether or not to continue.

If you decide to go on, in each week's meeting that follows you will center on a particular aspect of the journey with God, such as God's creative love, God's forgiving love, God's inviting and challenging love, and so on. You will be offered a set of handouts suggesting focus points for the following week's prayer. These may include Scripture passages or other inspirational material, and guidance on different approaches to prayer. The final meeting will be a chance to review the experience and reflect on the gifts received and shared.

A small charge is made for an open-door retreat, simply to cover the team's travel expenses and the cost of supplying the handouts. For those in need, financial assistance is sometimes available.

For more information about open-door retreats, contact the Cenacle Sisters through their Web site: www.cenaclesisters.org/nap.htm. If you choose to participate within a group setting, the retreat will normally extend over nine weeks. When it is over, you will almost certainly find that you are in touch with a wider network of fellow pilgrims than you would have thought possible when you first set out. For many people, the open-door retreat has become the start of a new, and radically less lonely, way of making the journey of life with God.

Faith-sharing meetings

For many Christians, the support of a small local group of fellow pilgrims is an essential part of their spiritual journey.

If you are feeling isolated in your faith journey, you may find support in inviting friends to your home to share something of their spiritual journey. Faith-sharing meetings of this kind can become a much cherished retreat time for all concerned. For many, this kind of private networking is a lifeline.

There are a number of ways in which such groups can function: prayer groups exist in many churches; house groups are becoming increasingly popular as a way of exploring faith questions more deeply; and Bible study and discussion groups flourish in many Christian churches and other establishments.

So what is different about a faith-sharing group, and what might you expect to find if you join one? The focus of a faith-sharing group is always upon the sharing of the members' lived experience of God's action and movement in their lives and hearts. To allow this experience to be shared in a nonthreatening way, certain principles apply

• The total confidentiality of everything that is shared must be assured. This principle, which is nonnegotiable, needs to be clearly understood and endorsed by every member from the start.

• The group meeting offers "safe space" in which people can share as much or as little of their experience as they wish. To this end, most of the meeting is spent in giving time to all members to open up anything at all they wish to share. While a person is sharing, the others engage in active listening, giving the sharer their complete attention.

Active listening means listening without any trace of
judgment, simply receiving what is being said in a spirit
of loving acceptance.

• When an individual has said what he or she wishes to
say, a brief period of silence is kept, to hold what has
been said in reverence and prayer. There is no discussion
and no attempt to set the person straight or to offer solutions to problems. There is no argument or questioning,
and the person sharing must never be interrupted. The
only possible exceptions to this are if a member of the
group needs to ask for clarification in order to understand what the person is saying or if time is becoming a
real problem.

• When all have shared what they wish to share, the
meeting may open up into a more general sharing, but
still with no discussion or attempts at therapy. The reason
for the ban on discussion is that the ethos of such gatherings is to operate from the heart and not from the head.
Discussions engaging reason and logic have an important
place in our journeying as, for example, in Bible study
groups, but the faith-sharing group is a place in which
heart speaks to heart.

• The meeting may end with shared prayer, silent or
vocal, and a chance to relax over a cup of tea or coffee.
Meetings normally take place in members' own homes,
ideally with a rotation of host and facilitator.

Why are faith-sharing groups so helpful if nothing is discussed and no solutions are offered? Perhaps the heart of the matter is that this kind of sharing provides a space in which we can reveal ourselves as we are to trusted fellow pilgrims, at least to an extent, and still continue to be unconditionally loved by them even if, at the "head level," they might disagree with our thoughts. In such a group, the ideal is to offer one another something of God's unconditional love and acceptance, and to enable one another to grow more fully into the people we really are. As soon as we offer to "fix" one another, we are virtually saying (in the language of transactional analysis), "You're not OK!" This runs completely against the spirit of faith sharing, which is based on the premise of "I'm OK; you're OK."

People who share their faith journey in groups such as this often describe the experience as that of walking on holy ground. When we are permitted to walk upon another person's holy ground of innermost experience, we "take off our shoes," step sensitively, and say nothing. Our silence honors the gift they are giving us, which is nothing less than a glimpse of the core of their being, where God is indwelling.

Practicalities. To create genuine oasis time in your own home, make sure that all members of the group agree to the ground rules for sharing experience. It is wise to make such a group strictly a listening group. This means that each person has an opportunity to share whatever he or she feels comfortable sharing and is assured of respectful silence. It can be helpful to light a candle or create some other focus upon which people can center themselves.

There should be no discussion, and certainly not any argument, arising from what is shared, and there should be no attempt to correct other people's views or resolve their problems. This is a sharing forum, not a therapy session. Discussion groups, prayer groups, and Bible study groups are, of course, all very valuable encounters, but they lie beyond the scope of this book and are not the same thing as sharing sacred space in quiet, nonjudgmental acceptance. In a group that does this, many people discover for the first time the gift of being genuinely and lovingly listened to. This is what turns a home group into a retreat space.

Retreats "behind closed doors"

If you are unfortunate enough to find yourself in prison, this needn't mean that a retreat is impossible. Increasingly, local spirituality networks are offering retreats in daily life to prison inmates. In this situation, the retreat guides arrange to visit the prison at regular intervals and conduct one-on-one meetings with each retreatant, just as in a standard retreat in daily life. Faith-sharing groups can also be established in a prison environment.

Practicalities. If you are interested in making a retreat in these circumstances, speak to your prison chaplain or contact Christian friends outside the prison to see if you

can find any information on local networks that might
be willing to approach the prison authorities to initiate
a retreat.

Another resource organization that may be able to help
you is the St. Dismas Prison Ministry, which for several
years has been bringing spiritual refreshment to the residents of the corrections system of Pennsylvania as well as
other parts of the country. Contact

Mr. Harry "Bud" Cope, St. Dismas Prison Ministry
1823 Service Lane
Monesson, PA 15062
(724) 684-4990
E-mail: budcope@att.net

Spirituality networks

During the past few years, the general understanding of
the word *spirituality* has moved from the exclusive and
somewhat esoteric domain of monks, nuns, and hermits
to being a concept that many people both inside and
beyond the visible church can and do relate to. There is
no doubt that a hunger for meaning in life and a serious
quest for an experience of the authentic mystery at the
core of our being is rapidly increasing and spreading.
Sadly, there is also a growing perception that organized
religion in its traditional forms is unable to satisfy this
hunger or facilitate this quest.

One of the ways in which people are beginning to get
in touch with the spiritual dimension of their being is

through the growing availability of retreats and quiet days, especially those that can be undertaken in daily life. Many people come away from an experience of retreat with a sharpened appetite for the search for God's presence and direction in their living. In time, such people gravitate together and form local networks.

Generally speaking, such spirituality networks are

• ecumenical;

• open equally to lay and ordained people;

• independent of the structures of any of the institutional churches;

• not for profit;

• willing to welcome you whether you have any contact with a Christian church or not.

A spirituality network may evolve for any number of reasons. Some of these networks are totally informal, while others are highly organized.

Active, organized networks. A support network may develop for people in a particular locality who are engaged in the giving of retreats to others or have a personal interest in developing their own spiritual lives and sharing their exploration with others. Such a local network will often facilitate retreats and quiet days for its members and will usually organize plenary gatherings at regular intervals. Larger networks also occasionally organize conferences.

Loosely structured information networks. A number of spirituality networks have developed around the country and overseas to help connect people who are seeking to make a similar kind of spiritual journey. Essentially, these networks are nothing more than a link of people in a particular area who know about each other and who may meet together from time to time to share ideas and inspiration. Usually someone among them will be responsible for keeping an up-to-date list of contact names and addresses. Some networks will follow a fairly structured approach in their meetings, while others will impose no structure at all.

Some local networks hold impressive databases of contact names, including details of an individual's particular expertise, extent of training, or special interests. If you are moving, for example, and hope to make contact with people in the new locality who are on your spiritual wavelength, you might do well by contacting a local spirituality network.

The cost of membership in a spirituality network varies considerably depending on the facilities it offers. If the network maintains a database of contact names and addresses, there will be a nominal charge to have your name included and receive a copy of the register, which also needs regular updating. Some networks produce a regular newsletter, advertising forthcoming retreats and quiet days and often including articles on spirituality and topics of general interest.

Examples of such networks include the following:

• The Ignatian spirituality networks. These networks enable people who are drawn to the Ignatian way to be in contact with each other. Some of them offer basic training in listening skills and accompanying others in prayer, and they all offer daily-life retreats, on request, to people in their regions.

• The Christian Life Community (CLC). This international organization, based on the spirituality of St. Ignatius, comprises a widespread network of small groups of between two and twelve people who meet regularly to share their experience of spiritual journeying. Each group is free to decide for itself how to structure its meetings and what material to use as a focus, but excellent material and guidelines are provided by the umbrella organization for those who wish to use it. The CLC is Jesuit-inspired, and each region has the benefit of a Jesuit chaplain. It is ecumenical and welcomes all who feel drawn to an Ignatian path and are seeking to deepen their life in God. Visit their Web site at www.clc-usa.org for more information about the organization or to receive their newsletter, *Harvest.*

• Third-order organizations. These are groups of people who feel drawn toward a particular spirituality (for example, the Carmelite way or the Franciscan way) and would like to be actively associated with the parent religious order without actually entering religious life. Associates, or third-order members, agree to live an appropriate lifestyle and usually take a vow, but they pursue their membership in the order within their normal daily life, family, and work environments. They meet regularly for prayer and to encourage and nourish growth in their chosen way.

• Julian Meetings/silent-prayer groups. Inspired by Dame Julian of Norwich, Julian groups meet regularly in circles of silent contemplative prayer. A Julian Meeting usually comprises a group of between six and fifteen people who gather in a private house, church, or chapel. If you are searching for a regular oasis of silent-prayer with like-minded people, a Julian Meeting or other silent-prayer group might be the place to look.

Spiritual connections for the computer literate

Perhaps you are home alone or seizing a few precious minutes while the baby is asleep or the children are watching TV. Maybe you are feeling trapped at your office desk, envying those who have time to pray. If you have Internet access, visit Sacred Space at www.jesuit.ie/prayer.

Wherever you find yourself, you will find this Web site a marvelous companion for your journey. The site is changed regularly and offers daily suggestions and insights that can be used in privacy at whatever time suits you.

Developed by the Irish Jesuits, this site provides an excellent and refreshingly accessible approach to daily meditation. Information on the screen guides you through a daily reflection, allowing you plenty of space to explore your own experience as you go.

Explore the Internet, too, for links with other spiritual pilgrims seeking e-mail contact. As always with random Internet connections, however, take care when corresponding with strangers, especially on matters as deep and significant as your journey with God.

Audio and video guides

Another way of deepening your solitary prayer might be to use a course on tape or video, which you may find by browsing in a good religious bookstore. Or you might try searching on-line sources such as Catholic Treasures (www.catholictreasures.com) or St. Joseph Communications (www.stjoe.com).

Self-directed retreats

Another response to the growing demand for retreat opportunities has come in the form of books that offer readers a programmed journey of prayer that can be undertaken in their own home and at their own pace. A book of this nature will, typically, suggest a theme or focus for your day's prayer, supported by scriptural texts and sometimes other material such as poems or suggestions for practical activities.

A suggested-reading list is given in appendix 2. Some of these books offer excellent guidance on making a home-based retreat. If you are doubtful as to whether a sustained retreat (either in daily life or in a retreat house) is right for you, you might find that using one of these books for a week or so will help you decide. You will benefit most from such a retreat, however, if you have a companion with whom you can reflect on how the prayer has been for you and where you feel God is acting in your life.

retreat companions, prayer guides, and soul friends

SO YOU HAVE DECIDED to make a retreat, either residentially or in daily life, and you have opted for an individually given retreat. This means that you are about to enter into the special relationship that exists between a retreatant and his or her retreat companion (if it is to be a retreat in daily life, this person might be called your prayer guide). If you have never experienced this kind of spiritual companionship before, you may have some questions about what to expect.

First of all, you may be reassured to know that, prior to a retreat, even the most experienced of retreat-makers has some mild apprehension as to who the guide will be and how the relationship will work out. First-time retreatants often imagine that this guide or director is going to be some kind of wonder being who knows all the answers and never sets a foot wrong in his or her own prayer life or Christian living. And they couldn't be more wrong!

One first-time retreatant told me what it was like meeting her retreat companion.

A dozen or so of us gathered in the church hall. By this time, the reality of the venture was beginning to dawn on me. Suppose I made a huge mess of it! Suppose I didn't know what to say to my companion! Suppose I just couldn't pray! All of a sudden, my enthusiasm turned to panic, and I nearly backed right out.

The retreat leader seemed to have a knack for dispelling our fears. He led us very gently into a time of stillness, helping us to experience practical ways of relaxing and sinking down to the deeper parts of ourselves. Then he explained how the retreat would work, how we would meet our companions once a week, and what those meetings would be like. Then came the crunch. We were assigned to our prayer companions. I glanced at the four "companions" who were sitting in the circle with us. Which one would I choose? Which one would I least want? The panic was rising again.

I needn't have worried. Barbara smiled across at me as my name was read out, and we went out together with her other three retreatants, to arrange times to meet and to get to know each other a little. Perhaps, I thought, it wouldn't be so impossible to share something of my prayer with her.

Before our first meeting, Barbara had given me a Scripture passage to use as a focus for prayer. I really had tried to make time for prayer each day, and sometimes I managed the silent fifteen minutes I had promised myself. Once I totally failed, and one day I had to cut the time short when my daughter came bursting in to tell me that the cat had been sick. I could only hope that God—and Barbara—would be forgiving!

However, there was never any question of reproach when things went awry, and I never once had the feeling that Barbara was judging me in any way. She just listened, and while I was with her, I got the feeling that I was the only person in her life. She gave me her undivided attention, and somehow that helped me, too, to attend wholeheartedly to what God had been doing in my life during the days between our meetings.

Soon, the daily time with God became something that I looked forward to. It gave me real nourishment and a baseline of inner peace that carried me through the rest of the day. I found that I wanted to pray more, and perhaps differently, and Barbara introduced me to ways of praying with Scripture that I'd never known about before.

COMPANION FOR THE JOURNEY

So who is this person who is going to accompany you, sharing with you this period of intensive prayer? What will he or she be like? Let us begin, if we may, by explaining a few key terms.

• **Retreat companion (or guide):** This term is often used to describe someone who accompanies someone on a residential retreat, often for a few days or weeks. In some retreat houses, the term *retreat director* might be used to describe this role.

• **Prayer guide (or companion):** This person accompanies someone making a daily-life retreat.

• **Soul friend (or spiritual director):** These terms are used interchangeably to describe a person who offers ongoing spiritual companionship by accompanying others over a longer period. We will explore the nature of this kind of relationship more fully at the end of this chapter.

In many ways the term *director* is misleading. No one is going to "direct" your retreat, let alone your ongoing life journey. There is only one Guide, one Director, in this encounter with God, and that is God's own Holy Spirit. (For this reason the term *prayer guide* is also a bit misleading; whatever else the prayer companion does, he or she will never attempt to "guide" or "direct" your prayer.) Nor is the journey you are about to make an exclusively "spiritual" one; it concerns the whole of you.

Whatever term is used, your retreat companion or guide is there to be with you, helping you to discern the movements of the Holy Spirit in your own life by simply reflecting back to you what seems to be happening. Your guide will accept and affirm you unconditionally (though without flattery). This is quite definitely a peer relationship, not an authoritarian one.

In a residential retreat, the retreat guide will have received training and be experienced in conducting an individually given retreat in a residential context. Such people are often doing this kind of work full-time. In a daily-life retreat your prayer guide will also have had some training in listening skills and in attending whole-heartedly, with empathy and without judgment, to another person's journey in faith. Most prayer companions have normal employment, are running homes and raising families, or are retired people. They offer their time as retreat guides in addition to their daily life commitments, often on a voluntary basis. They will not usually have had any professional training in spirituality, counseling, or psychology. They are simply listening companions and are often grappling with the same kinds of problems in life as you are.

The first meeting

You will discover who your guide will be during the first meeting of a retreat. This will happen either at the opening meeting of a daily-life retreat or on the first evening of a residential retreat. You will not normally have a choice of guide, though if you have real reason to feel that the appointed guide is the wrong person for you, you are free to say so and to ask the organizer whether it might be possible to change. This might be the case, for example, if you find you know the guide personally in some other context. Please bear in mind that once a retreat has begun it is very difficult to rearrange the guides and retreatants.

During an individually given retreat, the meeting between retreatant and retreat guide is an important landmark in the routine of the day or week. Most people look forward to these meetings as an opportunity to gather the fruits of the previous day's or week's prayer and focus on the best direction ahead. This is the opportunity to discern, together with your companion, what God seems to be doing in your prayer, what seems to be important for you, and what challenges and choices are beginning to crystallize. The discernment process is yours alone, but your companion can help by emphasizing what seems to be at the heart of your sharing. It is you who are singing your heart's song, but your companion will be able to echo to you the dominant chords of that song.

Sometimes there may be no great need to talk, and the meeting can be kept quite brief. At other times, you may need more time and space to open up important issues with your guide. Remember that there is no pressure at all in these conversations. They are simply a space shared with an accepting, nonjudgmental listener with whom you can explore anything you feel you want to explore. Your retreat is not an achievement course and there are no expectations. This type of retreat is individual in that it incorporates one-on-one sharing, but it is also "given." What is given is not a course or a program of direction or a schedule of prayer, but space, time, and wholehearted attention, together with gentle suggestions, if appropriate, as to how to move on in your next day's journey with God.

One religious sister summarized her recent retreat experiences with me as follows:

I liked most having a director, having unlimited time to just be, to pray, to do nothing. I need to change gears completely at times, and retreat time is the time I do that. A director challenges me to see things I haven't noticed so that my retreat times are usually challenging, sometimes uncomfortable; always at the end they come to a peaceful conclusion. I have been surprised by the fact that since I started directed retreats, the retreat experience lasts the whole year through and the theme of the retreat actually shapes my life until the next retreat.

What will I talk about with my retreat guide?

Most people, at the beginning of their first retreat, are convinced that they will never find enough to say to the retreat guide to fill the thirty or forty minutes scheduled for the one-on-one meetings. After the first meeting or two, most are wondering how on earth they are going to fit everything they want to say into such a relatively short time.

Let us begin with those worries. For one thing, the one-on-one meeting *may* last thirty minutes or more, but it *need* not. As the retreatant, it is for you to decide how long you want to stay in conversation with your guide, up to the maximum that time permits. If you have shared all that you wish to share in the first ten minutes and your guide senses that you are ready to end the meeting, then that's fine.

Having said that, most people find that they have more to say than they initially believed they would. For some, this may be the first time that another person has really listened to them and taken their feelings about their spiritual journey seriously. Such a listener encourages us to open up our deeper thoughts and feelings, our hopes and fears, and once trust has been established between the guide and the retreatant, the conversations begin to take on a life of their own. The problem is more likely to be the need to focus on what you really want and need to say, and to explore thoroughly what you most need to explore.

Appropriate material for these conversations is simply "anything and everything." The conversations with your guide are primarily focused on whatever has arisen in your prayer and reflection during the previous day. This prayer will be reflecting some aspect of your spiritual journey, which in turn is about the *whole* of you. There may be issues in your life or your relationships that come to mind in your prayer and that you would like to talk through with a sensitive listener. There may be doubts or hopes regarding your faith, or insights arising from what you have been praying about. Your guide will also be able to gently encourage you to explore any areas that appear to be important to you, and perhaps to open doors for you to take the conversation further.

What if, at the first meeting, you simply don't know where to begin? Probably your guide will have suggested something on which to focus your first day's prayer, which may in itself have sparked off some line of exploration in your heart. Otherwise, it might be helpful to share with the guide something of your faith journey thus far: the most obvious landmarks along the way and where it seems to be leading you right now. Your guide will help these early conversations to take shape by encouraging you to feel at ease and perhaps by opening up a few general questions in a nonthreatening way.

A Guide to Your Guide

It may help you to feel more at ease with your guide if you are aware of a few facts about guides in general.

Retreat guides are also retreatants themselves. They make their own retreats, usually on a regular basis, and know how it feels to be waiting nervously for a retreat to begin. They share their own spiritual journeys with a soul friend or spiritual director as well as with a supervisor. Later in this chapter, we will take a closer look at the role of this supervisor. However, it cannot be stressed too often that the strictest confidentiality is maintained in every reputable retreat house. Anything you share with your guide remains only between the two of you.

Most retreat guides find themselves in this role "by accident." People don't wake up one morning and decide that they will become retreat guides. Usually they are people who have found great challenge and joy in their own journeying with God and feel a desire to help others grow in their Christian life. When this happens, they may intensify their own searching, possibly by attending courses to help them listen more attentively, both to God's voice within themselves and to the ways in which God is active in others. Usually they will find that people are seeking them out, often informally, to share something of the spiritual quest. Then, when a retreat is planned, the organizers look around for people like this who might be willing to help on the team of companions or listeners. It is often to retreat guides' own surprise that they find themselves cast in that role.

All retreat guides should have had some training to help them develop their listening skills. If you wish to reassure yourself on this point, feel free to phone the retreat house and ask. Several things are emphasized during this training. The first, and most important, is the requirement for absolute confidentiality. You can be sure that nothing you share with your guide will ever go any further than the room wherein it is shared. Other aspects of the training include the nurturing of empathy, which means that your guide will "walk a mile in your moccasins," trying always to enter into your experience from your point of view. You will be unconditionally accepted and welcomed without any form of judgment. You can say whatever you want and express whatever views and feelings you need to without fear of offending your guide.

Training to become a prayer companion is offered in several locations in the United States and entails, usually, a course of evening meetings over eight or more weeks. Here the principles of active listening are introduced and practiced intensively, and the main aspects of the spiritual journey are explored. Trainees will usually also be asked to attend at least one residential weekend during which they will have the experience of giving someone else a short retreat while allowing another student to give them a retreat. Ideally, those showing a gift for this kind of companionship will then be asked to help as a trainee member of a team of prayer companions offering a daily-life retreat in the area. Follow-up training is often offered, which leads, in some cases, to more far-reaching courses and practical training under supervision.

A final aspect of the training will have enabled your guide to pick up those moments in what you are saying (or, indeed, in what you are not saying) that seem to indicate deep feeling or strong reaction, or some other sign of inner movement, and to reflect back to you what you were saying when that moment first occurred. This can be extraordinarily helpful in opening up for you an area that can now be safely explored. Often we don't know what we want to say until we hear ourselves say it. The guide is there to help you hear yourself say it.

The guide is fallible and may also be struggling with the big (and little) questions of faith. The most effective guides are often the ones who are most wounded themselves. Guides are not people who have got it all together but those who know how it feels to fall apart and surrender to God's remaking. Putting the guide on a pedes-tal, even unconsciously, will not be helpful for either of you. This will distract you from the purpose of your retreat, which is to come closer to God, not to the guide. Regard him or her as a friend who is also on the journey, also stumbling over the stones and stopping to admire the views.

Nevertheless, your guide will also be a person of prayer who takes *your* prayer and *your* journey seriously. For many people in retreat, it is a new experience to be able to share things about their journey with God and to have a listener alongside who is receiving "on the same wavelength."

Retreat guides may be male or female, lay or ordained, of any age, any denomination, and any cultural or ethnic background. Most commonly, however, people in the second half of life are engaged in this ministry and have acquired a lot of regular lived experience in addition to their own experience in prayer. What they are *not* is a race apart!

What Prayer Guiding Is . . . and Is *Not*

I often wonder, as I look around a group of people about to begin their individually given retreats, if they are asking the same question I frequently ask myself: "What do we think we are doing when we offer ourselves as companions to other people along their spiritual journey?"

Thankfully, they seldom voice this question aloud. However, there was one memorable occasion when it did come up. When asked "Does anyone have any questions?" a participant in a retreat in daily life stood up and addressed the team of prayer companions/prayer guides. "What makes you think you can teach us to pray?"

Needless to say, we were floored by the question, and this was especially true for me, as it was my first experience of prayer guiding following my training!

The question forced us to focus on what we are really doing—and more important, what we are not doing—when we accompany another person in prayer.

It might be worth taking a few minutes to look at some of the things that prayer guiding is *not* about:

• It is certainly not about teaching someone else to pray!

• It is not about trying to steer the other person's prayer in a particular direction.

• It is not about imposing any particular method of prayer or approach to prayer on another person.

• It is not an excuse to preach at the pilgrim, to share the prayer companion's own agenda, or to impart his or her own wisdom (real or imagined) to the pilgrim.

What it *is* about, however, is

• Being alongside other pilgrims as they reflect on their personal prayer and their journey with God.

• Listening intently and lovingly, and with full attention, to all that the pilgrim freely chooses to share.

• Reflecting back any moments from the sharing in which

the pilgrim seemed to be especially stirred in some way.

• Providing free and nonjudgmental space in which the pilgrim can explore these moments more deeply if he or she so chooses.

• Offering guidance on various approaches to prayer if the pilgrim requests this or appears to welcome it.

• Offering suggestions as to how the pilgrim might like to focus his or her attention in prayer in the days that follow the meeting, but leaving the pilgrim completely free to follow up on these suggestions or not.

As we have already said, the word *guide* is in many ways a misnomer. The relationship between you and your prayer companion is more like that of two people taking a walk through the countryside. One of these people is the discoverer, sharing the experience in words and gestures with the other. The other is there simply to be alongside, noticing the reactions and responses of the first, and affirming all that seems to be leading to growth and insight.

It might happen, during a country walk, that we stop to admire a particular view, or to notice some creature or plant along the path, or just to breathe in the fresh air. We may become aware of the weather, good or bad. We may move into conversation during this walk. Calmed by the serenity of the setting, we may open up issues that are active in our normal daily life, especially if we sense that we can really trust our companion.

These are also the kinds of things that might happen in our walk through the days or weeks of our retreat. The guide is not there, in any sense, to show us the way but to listen as we reflect on what is especially touching us or moving us in the current landscape of our lives. It is very valuable to have a companion in those moments when something we discover really captures our imagination and reveals something of where God is for us. Being able to share these things helps us to notice them more intently for ourselves. When another person plays back what he or she is hearing from us, it helps us to hear it anew for ourselves.

Someone once remarked, "How can I know what I mean until I hear myself say it?" This wisdom is one of the keys to so-called prayer guiding. The guide is there to provide the space for you to hear yourself saying what matters to you, and to reflect back what has been heard in a way that helps you to come closer to where God is active in it all.

Will a prayer guide be able to advise me on a particular problem?

A retreat guide or retreat director will have been trained, quite explicitly, not to try to solve problems. There are several excellent reasons for this.

First, retreat guides are simply companions. They are not normally trained to carry out psychotherapy, and they are not there as counselors. They are there to walk alongside you as a peer during a part of your spiritual journey. They will not step outside this range of competence, but if it is appropriate, they may sensitively suggest that you might benefit from specialized help such as relationship or bereavement counseling.

Second, the only authentic solutions to personal problems are those we discover for ourselves. It may well be that in the course of your retreat some new direction suggests itself to you or that your perspective on a problem changes, bringing new light. The retreat guide will simply listen to anything you wish to share and reflect back to you the way your own mind and heart seem to be moving. Often, when we speak about a problem with someone else, we hear ourselves in a new way and are able to understand the problem more clearly.

Nevertheless, you will certainly find retreats designed for people with a particular difficulty or those in a potentially painful situation in life. Examples include retreats specifically focused for the bereaved, for the divorced, or for those who are HIV-positive. The reason for this kind of focus is not to make the pain of difficult circumstances go away but to offer a safe space in which those in similar situations can come together, either in silence or to share their journeying with one another.

Sometimes quiet days or weekends are offered for people affected by some kind of addiction, such as alcoholism, or by eating disorders. These programs, while not offering any ready-made solutions, may sponsor workshops that allow you to explore your difficulty in a relaxed and accepting environment. If they are responsibly organized and run, their publicity will usually make it clear that they are not offering therapy.

I don't find it easy to open up to others.
Will I have to do this?

Whatever kind of retreat you choose, remember that it is *your* retreat, *your* special time with God. How you use this time is entirely up to you. Whether you choose a retreat in daily life, a faith-sharing meeting, or an individually given retreat in a retreat house, you should never feel pressured to talk about things you would rather keep to yourself.

If you really do find it difficult to talk openly with another person, to build up this level of trust and confidence, it might initially be better to choose a theme retreat rather than an individually given retreat. The former is an opportunity to deepen aspects of your Christian journey by listening to a speaker, following his or her suggestions for reflective exercises or approaches to prayer, and sharing with others in the group, or with the retreat leader, only if you specifically choose to do so. You will not normally experience any kind of pressure to share. If you do, you have every right to resist it.

In an individually given retreat, the focus is on your individual prayer. You will therefore be invited to share your reflections on your prayer with your guide to the extent that you feel comfortable, and no further.

It is the task of the retreat guide to nurture an atmosphere of trust that encourages you to be as open as possible. The retreat guide is also trained to be sensitive to the reactions of the retreatant, to read and be responsive to unspoken signals. The guide should be able to sense where you are open to sharing and where you would rather hold back. Every guide knows that some

retreatants will choose to share very little, while others
will be almost unstoppable. People are very different, and
you will not be expected to be any other than who you
are. If by any chance a guide misjudges your intentions or
your comfort level, it will be helpful for you to be as
direct as possible in stating your preferences.

Sometimes when we are reflecting deeply on what matters most in our lives, we reach a point where we feel we
really want to go on in our explorations but don't quite
know how or don't yet have the courage to do so. If your
guide detects such a moment, he or she may very gently
encourage you to "unpack" a little. This is usually done by
using open questions that don't presuppose any specific
kind of answer, or indeed, any answer at all. He or she may
reflect back something that you yourself have said. It is
then entirely up to you to follow up on this invitation or
not. The guide won't mind either way and will not pursue
anything that you don't pick up on for yourself. Silence is a
totally acceptable response at any stage, and so is a simple
statement that you don't want to say any more about a particular matter. Remember that in every conversation with
your guide, it is you who sets the agenda.

Should I be on guard against
being pressured or brainwashed?

If you choose your retreat house carefully and prayerfully,
asking for guidance from people who have some experience making a retreat or who have themselves visited a
retreat house you are considering, you will not suddenly

find yourself in the clutches of a coercive organization bent on getting you to think and act as they do. No bona fide retreat house exists to exert any kind of pressure on its guests. This attitude would run counter to the whole idea of making a retreat, and it would be anathema to any sincere retreat guide. The purpose of all retreat houses is to allow individuals to explore their relationships with God in a setting that is quiet, supportive, and conducive to prayer and reflection.

In the extremely unlikely situation that you *do* find yourself in a place that seems to have a hidden agenda, you are free to leave it at any time and without giving any reason for your departure. If this should ever happen, and the retreat house in question was advertised in a public forum, such as the Retreats International Web page or in a journal or magazine, it would be good for you to respectfully describe your experience to whomever runs the advertisement. Few promoters of the retreat experience would knowingly endorse any house seeking to exert influence of this kind on its guests.

Nor should your retreat guide try to persuade you to follow a particular line of thought or make a decision in a particular way. Retreat guides are trained not to get between God and the retreatant, and certainly never to seek to impose their own pet theories or allegiances on another person. If you really feel that a retreat guide is trying to exert some kind of pressure on you, it is your right and your duty to protect yourself. It would be important first to voice your misgivings to the retreat guide in person, if you can. If you feel uncomfortable confronting the guide, you are free to approach the person who is coordinating the retreat. You are also free simply not to meet with your guide and to let God guide your retreat without any outside help. You do not need to give any reason for your choice. If the guide has a problem with this, it is not something about which you need concern yourself.

Thankfully, these scenarios are unlikely. When you enter into retreat, however, you are making yourself rather vulnerable before both God and your guide. God will never abuse this vulnerability and neither will the vast majority of guides. Generally speaking, the interaction with a guide is self-regulating. Most people will only share what they feel comfortable sharing, and most of us have a strong sense of whom we can trust and to what extent. We will open our hearts when we sense the presence of God in the guide, and we will close them when we do not. This is the best protection against any kind of manipulation.

Remember, too, that the guide will be receiving regular supervision, and the supervisor will be watchful for any signs of a hidden agenda in the guide. It is part of the supervisor's job to help the guide to acknowledge this and deal with it before it can affect anyone else.

What will my retreat guide expect of me?

Even though we may have made many retreats before, it is understandable, and perhaps inevitable, that we feel a bit anxious about our first encounter with the retreat guide. Who will it be? Will we hit it off together? Will I make a fool of myself? The questions go round and round in our heads.

We may need to turn this question around and ask ourselves what *we* think the guide will expect of us. In reply to ourselves, we may discover that we are afraid, for example, that the retreat guide may be expecting us

• To be at a so-called mature stage of our spiritual journey

• To know what we want

• To be familiar with different forms of prayer

• To be in the habit of regular personal prayer

• To be very sure of our faith, and without doubts

• To be able to articulate our deepest feelings, and so on . . .

Any or all of these things may come to haunt us as we approach a retreat. Let us lay them all to rest with the assurance that no retreatant (including retreat guides themselves when they make their own retreats) would ever get a very high score on expectations such as these. Let us look at these common misconceptions one by one:

• There is no such thing as a "mature Christian." We are all beginners on the spiritual journey, and Jesus assures us that being "as little children" is the best possible way to be.

• Rare are the individuals who know what they want. If they do, this may be because their mind-set is closed to the possibility of growth and discovery. Not to know what you want is to be open to discovering layer upon layer of your desires until you reach the depths where your own desires meet God's desires for you.

• There are as many forms of prayer as there are people seeking to pray. Your guide will accompany you wherever you are.

• Regular personal prayer is an ideal that many long for and few attain in practice. A retreat is a time to explore our *desire* for prayer, not to demonstrate our imagined achievements.

• Doubts are often the gateway to new growth, while fixed certainties can prevent that growth. It has been said that the opposite of faith is not doubt, but certainty.

• The deepest feelings usually defy words. Your guide will be alongside you when words fail, reading the signals of your heart. The stumbling searcher will often come closer to his own truth than the smooth verbalizer. God speaks through the gaps in our self-expression, and your guide will be tuned in to those gaps as much as she is tuned in to the things you say aloud.

• We have almost all grown up in a culture that measures our personal value to a certain extent by our achievements.

It would be naive to think that we can shed this mind-set instantly when we are on retreat. Really, however, that is what we have to do. As soon as you step over the threshold into your place of retreat, you are stepping back from the world that measures you by your qualifications and certificates. The simple fact is that your retreat guide will not be expecting anything of you.

Every retreat guide will start from the premise that this is *your* time and *your* retreat. It is space in which to explore your personal relationship with God in whatever way you feel most comfortable. The guide will *hope for* an openness of heart toward God and toward whatever possibilities unfold during your prayer. There will be no expectations at all about your familiarity with Scripture, with theology, with the practices of any particular tradition, or with prayers of one type or another. The guide will not expect any predictable pattern of prayer and will be completely open if, instead of praying with the material he or she has suggested, you choose to spend the entire afternoon playing the guitar, drawing pictures, or playing with clay. You are free to burst into song or to burst into tears, to sing with praise or scream in anger. The guide is trained to expect the unexpected and to move along with whatever may happen.

How can I make the most of my meetings with my retreat companion?

If you are making an individually given retreat, whether in seclusion or in daily life, you will be meeting your retreat guide on a regular basis for the duration of the retreat. These meetings are invaluable opportunities to grow in your discernment of what God is doing in your life and of where God is calling you to be. The following guidelines may help you to ensure that these meetings are as fruitful as possible:

• *Be punctual.* Your guide may be seeing several other retreatants and will be relying on your adherence to the time schedules involved. During a retreat in daily life, be sure to let your guide know ahead of time if you are unable to attend one of the meetings. This common courtesy will allow your guide to use his or her time most effectively and to be as flexible as possible in rescheduling your session.

• *Come prepared.* Go through any notes you have made during your periods of reflection since you last met with your guide. In much the same way that you review an individual prayer period, you can review your notes to see what themes, concerns, moods, or reactions have prevailed since your last meeting. The more you are able to focus ahead of time on what really matters to you, the less likely you are to get to the end of the meeting without having said what you really needed to say.

• *Be as open as possible with your guide.* Your guide will be standing alongside you, helping you to discern where God has been especially present to you and what this presence means for you. Guides are not mind readers, though they should be able to read body language. Tell it like it is and not as you imagine the guide (or God!) would like it to be. The guide may say very little during the meeting. This isn't a sign of lack of interest, but an indication of good, nonintrusive companionship. At the end of the meeting, listen attentively to whatever the guide does have to say and take on board anything that rings true with you.

• *Try to retain a feel for the passage of time during the meeting.* It is the responsibility of the guide to keep the meeting to the set time, but you can help by not leaving the most important issues to the last five minutes. Remember that the guide will probably have another appointment following your meeting, and if your meeting runs overtime, someone else will be getting short measure.

What if I don't feel comfortable with my retreat guide?

The opening meeting of the retreat has taken place, and you have been given the name of your retreat guide. Whether yours is a retreat in daily life or a residential, individually given retreat, you will probably not have been allowed to choose your own guide. Understandably, you may have some reservations about how you will get on with the person who is to accompany you through your retreat and with whom you will be sharing something of the things that matter most to you in life.

One of the odd things about retreat making and retreat giving is that when two people are walking together on the holy ground of one person's experience in prayer and in life, the normal tendencies to like or dislike each other seem not to apply. People who might be perceived as irritating if you met them at a party give no such impression when they are sharing the deeper reaches of their hearts. There is an almost instinctive positive regard for a person who is entrusting something of their deepest dreams to you. It sounds like a cliché, but it also happens to be true. Perhaps something of God's unconditional love shapes the interaction between two people who are consciously seeking God's way together.

It may happen, however, that when you move into the second or third day of a retreat and begin to become aware of the issues that are arising in prayer, you may not like what you see. A natural psychological defense in this situation is to project (or transfer) any negative feelings onto the person nearest at hand, which will usually be your retreat guide. A sensitive guide will be able to deal with this and will stay alongside you, uncomplainingly, while you and God explore the painful places.

Even so, you might be tempted to decide that your retreat guide is the real cause of the problem, and to look for an escape route. However, if the reason for the discomfort lies with you and your agenda rather than with the guide, then changing to a different guide will not solve anything. Often this kind of problem goes away as the retreat progresses. Through the grace of prayer, the retreatant begins to look more honestly at his or her issues and stops transferring the negativity to the guide. The guide who seemed like a stumbling block at the beginning of the retreat is in the end often valued as a stepping-stone.

Perhaps the best advice is to exercise caution before rejecting a particular guide. Try to express your feelings honestly and trust that the guide will be able to cope with this. Be patient and see how things go. If there is a genuine impasse, the matter can be referred to the retreat administrator. Sometimes a change can be offered, though this isn't easy to organize without disrupting the retreats of other people.

Above all, let it be a matter for prayer. Sometimes the people who irritate us initially become the grain of sand in our oyster that eventually forms the pearl of great price.

Your Retreat Guide's Supervisor

Whatever type of retreat you make, whether in daily life or in a retreat house, over a day or over thirty days, your retreat guide will have a supervisor. The guide will meet with this supervisor regularly to open up any issues that arise from his or her work with the retreatants. This supervision meeting between your guide and his or her supervisor is strictly about the agenda of your guide, and under no circumstances will a guide ever divulge anything of what an individual retreatant has shared.

Supervision has been described as a place in which retreat guides can open up doors that have so far been closed in their own journeying. A retreatant may inadvertently knock on one of those closed doors so that the guide has an inner reaction to that knock. Perhaps something has been mentioned that the guide herself is trying to avoid acknowledging in her own life. A good guide will never reveal this to the retreatant but will observe his or her own reactions and raise them with the supervisor.

Ideally, the supervisor will be from a different area or parish and will have no personal contact with or knowledge of any of the retreatants. Even if this is not the case, when in supervision the guide has a responsibility to conceal the identity of everyone he or she is accompanying. If the guide does need practical guidance in order to help a retreatant, he or she will seek that guidance with utmost discretion, changing details as necessary so as to protect the privacy of the retreatant.

While the focus of the supervision meeting is the companion's experiences, not the retreatant's, both participants directly benefit from this supervision. If it happens that the guide is reacting to something the retreatant has been sharing, this can be taken off-line, so to speak, and dealt with in supervision so that it is less likely to impact the dialogue with the retreatant.

Anyone who is offering ongoing soul friendship or spiritual direction should have both a supervisor and a soul friend or spiritual director of his or her own. In the field of spiritual companionship, no one can give to others what they are not receiving themselves.

SPIRITUAL DIRECTION
AND SOUL FRIENDSHIP

Spiritual direction or soul friendship is an ongoing process, usually carried out in the course of daily life rather than in a retreat situation.

The Celts have a saying that "a person without a soul friend is like a body without a head." The ancient ministry of soul friendship is about ongoing spiritual companionship. In the Celtic tradition, the soul friend, or *anam cara,* was considered essential to any serious journey of the soul. Today the ministry of soul friendship—also known as spiritual direction, mentoring, or companionship—is growing and flourishing again.

What makes a soul friend? Well, it is probably true to say that soul friends are both born and made. Anyone whom others seek out as a companion along the way will usually have certain gifts, which might, for example, include the following:

• The ability and the desire to give undivided, loving attention to the person who is sharing the journey.

• The ability to hold all that is shared in total confidence.

• The gift of empathy, allowing the soul friend to walk awhile in the pilgrim's shoes. Empathy is not the same as sympathy. Empathy means that the listener steps into the place of the speaker and is thus able to see things from the speaker's point of view.

• The gift of unconditional positive regard, enabling the listener to be present and accepting of the speaker even if the speaker is expressing opinions or feelings that are radically different from the listener's own.

• The ability to be oneself, without putting on masks or hiding behind false images. The natural soul friend will be at ease with himself, with no discrepancy between how he projects himself and how he really is. He will be willing to face, with God and with his own soul friend, those parts of himself that he might prefer to ignore.

• The gift of prayerfulness. No one can accompany another on their journey of prayer unless they are prayerful themselves. A soul friend will usually be of a contemplative disposition, able to accompany another without interfering.

This gifting can be summed up in a comment sometimes made about a good soul friend: "When you are with her she makes you feel as though you are the only person in the world and that she has all the time in the world to be alongside you."

Soul friends may be male or female and are often laypeople with no special status in the institutional church. They usually find themselves drawn into this ministry simply because people seek them out and entrust to them the sacred space of their soul's journey.

Often, though not always, these gifts will have been encouraged and developed by some kind of training. The gifted soul friend, even untrained, will be sought after. The trained soul friend without the gifting will not.

Finding your soul friend

It is you, the pilgrim, who must choose your soul friend—not the church, not the bishop, not the parish priest, but *you*. You may know of people in your area who are willing and able to accompany others on their journeys of faith. You may decide to seek out one such person and ask whether he or she would be willing and able to accompany you.

Often you will gravitate to the right person almost intuitively. Look at your own circle of friends and acquaintances. Perhaps you already know someone who is on your wavelength spiritually, someone who is a person of prayer, who can listen gently and nonjudgmentally, without being tempted to off-load an agenda onto you. Often the right soul friend is found in an unexpected quarter.

If you feel you know who might be right for you, begin by asking this person how he or she feels about offering you this ministry. Remember that there is a limit to how many pilgrims a soul friend can reasonably accompany, so if the answer is no, don't take it personally; instead, ask if he or she might be able to suggest another person. If the answer is yes, make arrangements about how often you will meet. This varies, of course, from person to person. People who are meeting a soul friend regularly may choose to meet every few weeks, every few months, or even just once a year. The length of these meetings again depends on what suits you both, but an hour would be a typical duration.

The friendship begins

A common practice at the beginning of an arrangement to meet with a soul friend is to suggest a trial period of about three meetings. That way, each of you is able to reflect on the relationship and decide whether it would be fruitful to take it further.

Some people ask for some financial compensation for the time they give to this ministry. Others do not. This often depends on whether or not the person has any other means of support and whether or not they have to pay for their own spiritual direction and supervision. You need to establish expectations in this regard at the outset.

It is customary for the pilgrim to go to the soul friend's home or office for the session of spiritual direction, though a soul friend will often be willing to visit people who are housebound or without transportation.

The relationship between pilgrim and soul friend is, for the most part, one-way. The pilgrim shares whatever she wishes with the soul friend, but the soul friend will not normally share much of his own journeying unless this will help to set the pilgrim at ease or add any genuine clarification to a particular issue. This is not a sign of distrust or secrecy on the part of the soul friend but part of the process of practicing empathy. He cannot walk in your shoes if he is preoccupied with his own!

As is often the case, the benefit you will derive either from a retreat or from ongoing spiritual companionship depends to a great degree on how much effort you are willing to invest in it. The next chapter offers some suggestions on how to prepare for your retreat experience so that when you arrive you will be ready to receive whatever it is God wants to give you during that time.

how should i prepare for my retreat experience?

A RETREAT IS a special time. It is an appointment with the deepest part of yourself, where God is indwelling. You will probably be thinking about it for weeks ahead of the actual date. As for a vacation but even more so, you will be making advance preparations in your head and in your heart. In this section, we will look at a few things you might like to consider while thinking ahead.

PREPARING FOR A RETREAT IN DAILY LIFE

If you are planning to make a retreat in daily life, it may help to take into account the following questions:

• Are you familiar with the way such a retreat is usually run? Much of this was covered in the last two chapters (see the "Retreats in daily life" section in chapter 3 and the explanation of prayer companions in chapter 4). These chapters will give you some idea of what to expect from your retreat and your companion.

• Are you familiar with the venue for the opening meeting of the retreat? Have you set aside the time to go to it?

• Have you made whatever arrangements are necessary to allow you to meet with your prayer companion on a regular basis? An exact schedule will be decided at the first meeting. Most prayer companions are prepared to be fairly flexible, though of course they will often have to arrange your meeting times around the needs of their own work and family situations.

PREPARING FOR A RESIDENTIAL RETREAT

If you are planning to make a residential retreat, your practical preparations may be more extensive:

• If you have family commitments, have you made arrangements for someone to look after children, elderly or infirm relatives, and/or pets while you are away from home?

• Do you know what to expect when you arrive at the location of your retreat? Much of this has been addressed in chapter 2. Contact the retreat house if you have additional questions.

• Do you know what time to arrive and what you need to take with you? The retreat house will normally give you information about arrival and departure times well in advance. If you are unsure, just give the retreat house a call to check. Some suggestions as to what you might need (and might not need) to take with you are offered below.

• Have you notified the retreat house of any special requirements you may have? For example, do you need wheelchair access or have other mobility needs (such as a room on the ground floor or easy access to a bathroom)? Do you have any dietary needs or hearing or visual impairments? Your needs may depend to a certain extent upon the type of retreat you have chosen. For example, in a theme retreat, someone with a hearing impairment may need to be seated close to the speaker.

What if my family is hostile to the idea of my making a retreat?

It can happen that an individual feels strongly the need to make some kind of retreat, but other members of the family are less than enthusiastic. There may be several reasons for this.

Probably the person most likely to meet resistance to her hopes of making a retreat is the mother of the family. And much of the resistance may stem from the fact that while Mom is away, the rest of the family will have to fend for themselves. Indeed, it can be extremely difficult to get a family organized sufficiently to allow the "bread baker" to move out for a few days, but it may also prove to be a growth point for all concerned.

For a working parent and his or her family, making a retreat often means that the annual family vacation will have to be curtailed. Such a decision may be interpreted as a selfish desire on the part of one family member to do his or her own thing at the expense of the family vacation. Balancing priorities in this situation can be very difficult. If the situation is genuinely either-or, it may be necessary to postpone a separate residential retreat until the children are older. Childhood and family vacations slip by all too quickly, and "babies don't keep"! On the other hand, if a time in retreat might help to illuminate some domestic or professional difficulties, the sacrifice of a week's vacation might prove to be a sound investment for the whole family. In this situation you might do well to consider making a daily-life retreat rather than a residential retreat.

Here are the experiences of one mother:

I was thrilled at first when the prospect of a retreat was mentioned at the faith-sharing group I belong to. I had wanted to make a retreat for as long as I knew that such things happened.

I didn't really have much of an idea what it would entail, but I knew it was something I wanted to do.

I remember arriving home that night and telling the family my news. "There's going to be a retreat," I said. "I hope there's no objection to my taking part."

I could see from their faces that they were not impressed.

"What's a retreat, when it's at home?" my teenage son muttered rather sullenly from the depths of his pile of homework.

"Mommy, you're not going away, are you?" my younger daughter cried, with panic in her voice.

My husband just looked at me over the top of the newspaper. "Another fad," I thought I heard him thinking. "She'll get over it."

Despite her initial misgivings, Ann persevered and went on the retreat. Later, she writes of the experience:

Those six weeks were a major turning point in my life. Perhaps that was when my journey with God moved beyond "religion" into "relationship." When the children are a bit older, I hope to go away on a residential retreat. Meanwhile, I will certainly be joining in the next daily life retreat. And there will be another one—all of us who made the retreat are determined to make sure of that!

It can also happen, in close relationships, that one or the other of the people concerned needs to make a retreat because his or her spiritual journey is deepening and growing. This in itself can appear very threatening to the other person involved. We all evolve at our own pace, and two people who are otherwise deeply committed to each other can find themselves out of sync with each other's growth at various stages of their relationship. This kind of mismatch requires very delicate handling if the legitimate needs of each person are to be honored. Here are a few suggestions:

• If you encounter serious resistance at home and sense that this is about more than merely "Who will cook my supper when you're away?" consider making a retreat in daily life first. This will give you space to reflect on your journey, to share it with a prayer companion or prayer guide, and to grow in your own personal inner freedom. It may also help to demonstrate that your spiritual journey is not as threatening to the other as it first seemed. You may find that a daily-life retreat will help to free you from your own fears, to discern where you need to confront any resistance and where it would be more fruitful to accept it and work with it, remembering that everything is always moving on, and this year's blocks may become next year's gateways.

• It might be possible to make a retreat away from home for just a short period at first—maybe a weekend or a few days only. It is much easier to organize a family to run on its own for two or three days than for six or eight days. And if you go away on retreat and return to the family enriched and in deeper harmony with yourself (as you almost certainly will!), they will see for themselves that what they feared was not so fearful after all, and it may be possible to make a longer retreat at a later stage.

• If the root of the resistance is a fear that you may be "changed" or "manipulated" while you are away, it might be worth suggesting that both of you make a short retreat together. Some retreat houses offer special weekends for couples. Sharing the experience in this way, at least initially, can help to dispel any fears there may be.

• If one of the people in a close relationship is resistant in general to any prolonged absence by the other, or any separate activity, then there is a problem that goes beyond merely the question of making a retreat. Where one person is looking for space to explore his or her life questions independently, and the other is finding this deeply threatening, there may be a need for some form of relationship counseling. If you find yourself in this situation and feel that you really need the space that a residential retreat can give, it may take a lot of courage to make up your mind to go. Though there are no guarantees, a genuinely spiritual retreat, with a sensitive retreat guide, may give you the very space you need to step back, to look at whatever problems there may be, and to move forward in a more enlightened way when you return home.

Prepare to Embrace the Experience

Whether your retreat is to be residential or in daily life, a few preparations will help you to derive the maximum benefits from the experience.

Sister Kathryn Hermes, author of *Beginning Contemplative Prayer,* offers this practical advice:

Be rested beforehand. . . . Begin to take time to walk, slow down, read a little extra, do some things that relax you. Give your mind time to just be blank. Don't go on retreat with any expectations. Don't give God any demands or ultimatums. Just say, "Here I am, Lord." Don't take a lot of books to read. Give God some time to talk. . . . Find a prayer symbol that you like: a candle, a crucifix, anything visual that you can bring with you to focus on when you feel restless.

Personal retreat preparations

The way an individual prepares for a retreat is a very personal matter. Nevertheless, here are a few general suggestions that may be helpful.

If you are going to make a retreat in daily life, the most important part of your preparation might be to reflect on how, where, and when you are hoping to make your regular time of prayer. Your day may already be so busy that it isn't yet clear how you are going to make time for prayer, but the value of your retreat will be diminished if you can't take regular time for prayer in a fairly deliberate way, preferably every day but at least three or four times during the week.

Some people are able to arrange a fairly predictable schedule during the regular school week or workweek, while realizing that some adjustments will be inevitable on the weekends when the whole family is at home and a different order of events prevails. Some guidelines for this process are offered later on in this chapter, but in preparation you might like to consider the following:

• *How much time can you give to prayer each day, or on a regular basis?* Do be realistic! Ten minutes of time alone in prayer, faithfully adhered to day by day, is much more effective than high hopes of half an hour a day that you almost never manage. As with any other form of exercise, setting unrealistic goals can result in your feeling discontented with yourself, making you that much more likely to give up on the whole thing.

• *Where can you go to pray?* Ideally, prayer time should be in a place where you can be alone and uninterrupted for as long as you have decided to set aside. In the midst of family life this can be difficult. Some people choose to go out to a nearby park or into a church for their prayer time. Others find it possible to switch off and focus on God while they are making their commuter journey by bus or train. You may be able to find a few quiet moments in your own home, perhaps in the early morning or after the children have gone to school or to bed. If so, choose a place in the house that is to be your prayer space. Maybe you could keep a candle there, with your Bible or some token of your desire to pray. Use a chair that is straight-backed and supportive but also comfortable. Some people prefer to use a prayer cushion or prayer stool. Having a special place like this will make it easier for you to move readily into a relaxed and prayerful state of mind. It will also help your time of prayer to become a daily joy.

• *What time of day best suits your routine?* Some people are natural larks and others are nightingales. Many find that the early morning, before the rest of the household is awake, is the perfect time for prayer, setting the whole day off to a good start. For others, the very idea of rising at 6:00 A.M. is a nightmare. Listen to your own body clock and try to find a time when you are alert but able to relax for the time you have allocated to prayer. Night prayer is a lovely habit to form, but you may find that you fall asleep in the middle of your meditation. Remember, too, that prayer can permeate your whole day, consciously and unconsciously. More guidance on keeping prayer alive in this way will be offered later in this chapter.

Many of these same guidelines also apply if you are planning to make a residential retreat. Your guide will help you to organize your day in retreat, incorporating prayer, reflection, rest, and exercise in a balanced way. Because there are no external distractions, you will probably find it much easier to make space and time for prayer. As regards the place for prayer, you will have a number of choices: your own room, the chapel(s) and quiet room(s) in the house, and the countryside outside the doors.

Questions to consider beforehand

Before making your retreat, you might like to spend a little time reflecting on these questions:

• *What am I bringing with me into this retreat?* Be aware of any issues that are in your life right now, either positive or negative. Don't try to resolve them and don't make judgments about them. Just be aware of them. Don't assume that the retreat will center on these issues, as God may have other plans for his time with you at the oasis. Simply being aware of what baggage you are carrying may help to clear the pathway for the journey of prayer that lies ahead.

• *What am I actually hoping for from this retreat?* How would you answer if God were to ask you, "What would you most like me to do for you right now?" It is good to be aware of your heart's desire, however unlikely you think its fulfillment may be. Simply carry your desires into your prayer and into your retreat, and if you wish to do so, share them with your prayer companion.

The most helpful advice I ever received regarding prayer in retreat was given to me just before I left home to go on my first residential retreat. The advice was this: "No predictions!"

Anticipate distractions

If you have never made a retreat, it might be difficult for you to imagine how you might get through a week without engaging in your favorite diversions, such as listening to the radio, watching television, or reading a novel or two. Should you pack your Walkman? Or must you be "holy" the entire time you are on retreat?

To answer this question, we must first decide for ourselves what "being holy" means. It has a great deal to do with wholeness, which in turn is pretty inclusive. Nevertheless, in most retreat houses there is a sense of holiness that isn't as obvious in our daily lives. Some of this atmosphere of holiness is authentic. Retreat houses are places where prayer regularly happens, where people are truly searching for, and experiencing, what lies deepest in their hearts. This is not brought about just by the people who are living there this week, or this year, but is often an atmosphere that has been generated over decades or even centuries of prayerful withdrawal and renewal.

Then again, some of this "holy atmosphere" can be less authentic and may be the result of imposed or affected piety that people put on like a cloak because they think they should behave in a particular way in a retreat house. There is nothing wrong with giving this appearance, *unless* it becomes an aim in itself, distracting us from the purpose of the retreat, which is always to grow more fully into our true selves before God.

Perhaps the first thing to reflect upon is whether the everyday occupations we engage in are any less holy than the attitudes we adopt when we are "officially praying." Reading a novel, listening to music, and watching a good play can all lead us closer to God as surely as an hour of adoration in the chapel. In principle, therefore, there is nothing wrong with doing any of these things during a retreat, provided they are not distracting you—or anyone else—from the underlying desire to engage with God more deeply than might be possible in everyday life.

On the other hand, it is often easier to pick up a book or tune in to the radio or television than it is to be still and allow yourself to sink deep into the core of your being, where you will be better able to discern the action and movements of God in your heart and in your life. If, during an individually given retreat, you feel the need to read or to engage in other activities such as listening to a Walkman or watching television, it might be wise to talk through your feelings with your retreat guide. He or she will be able to help you discern whether these activities, in your particular case, are more potentially helpful or distracting.

The empty space that results from not reading, not listening to the radio, and not watching television may feel daunting, and the temptation to fill it up may be overwhelming at first. Remember that not doing these things makes a space in which God may reveal himself, and think twice before putting up any unnecessary roadblocks. Keep yourself as open as possible to the power of prayer and uninterrupted stillness, not because others will expect it of you, but because it is in that stillness and apparent emptiness that you are most likely to discover what you have come on retreat to find.

Appreciating the gift of silence

Silence is expected or requested in many retreats, particularly individually given retreats. Many quiet days and theme retreats also reserve time for silent prayer and reflection.

This kind of silence should not be regarded as an imposition, a discipline, or some form of ascetical practice. Rather, it is a gift that we offer to each other as people seeking a place to be still and to reflect on the presence and action of God in our lives. When we offer each other a time of silence, we are also offering the gift of sacred space, in which we undertake not to disturb each other's quiet by talking. The silence respects and protects each person's space and privacy, and ensures that no one retreatant can undermine another's retreat by talking about his or her own agenda.

Silence can be disturbing in its own way, of course. Some people find a silent retreat very challenging. Without the comforting distractions of normal background noise or of radio and television, we come closer to recognizing our true selves, our real needs, our dependencies, and the true nature of our relationship with God. The whole point is to break free of the many chains to which we may find we are more attached than we thought we were, to move forward to wherever God within us is inviting us.

The silence in a retreat house has a special quality, and most people discover very quickly that it is not a threatening silence at all. On the contrary, it creates an ambience that bonds the retreatants and their guides closer together without any actual intrusion on the individuals' personal space. When we cannot use words to greet each other or to express our needs (at meals, for example) or to convey empathy, we are obliged to use a deeper kind of language. We become much more aware of people's gestures, their facial expressions, the language of their eyes, and so on. As a result of this awareness, we become much more sensitive to their needs.

Some people feel, at the end of a silent retreat, that they know their fellow retreatants more deeply than if they had been able to speak with them in the normal way. The gift of silence has led them, in ways they could not and do not need to express, not only to the core of their own being but also to the core of the being of those around them.

People deal with silence in different ways. If you are not used to any silence at all in your life, it might be wise to try a first-time retreat for two or three days before you commit yourself to a week or more in silence. In a taster retreat such as this you will have several hours of silence each day, but there will also be opportunities to talk and to share your experience with others. This will give you a sense of how you personally react to the effects of silence.

As a simple though not exhaustive test of how your particular personality might deal with being alone in silence for several days, you could try asking yourself these questions:

• *When I am with a crowd of people at a party or in some kind of group activity, do I tend to come more alive the more I am with them, or do I find I need to withdraw at some stage to get a bit of quiet and re-collect myself?* If the latter is more descriptive of you, your natural way of gaining the energy you need for living is more likely to be found in a source of quiet solitude than in a crowd of people. It might suggest that

you are a natural introvert, in which case you will probably
deal well with silence and benefit from it even though it
may seem strange in the beginning.

• *When I find myself alone for any length of time, do I tend to
come more alive, or do I eventually feel a pressing need to be
with others again and rejoin the hustle and bustle of social life?*
If you identify more with the latter, you probably gain
energy from being with other people and from your
interactions with them. In this case, extensive solitude
may eventually diminish your energies. This would be the
pattern of a natural extrovert, who might find it harder to
deal with the extended silence of a secluded retreat.

These two patterns are equally valid. God deals with
his creatures as they are, extrovert or introvert. It may be
wise to consider choosing the kind of retreat that more
closely matches your natural patterns. If you feel that you
veer more toward the extrovert model, you might find a
theme retreat a better first step. If you feel that the introvert model more accurately describes your character, a
silent retreat may suit you very well.

Whatever your personality type, your retreat guide will
help you make the most of your retreat, including the
times of quiet.

What if I fall apart in solitude?

Solitude isn't something everyone finds comfortable.
This isn't a fault but a matter of personality type.

Generally speaking, an extrovert personality gains energy from being with people and can find it draining to be alone, especially in silence. An introvert personality is more likely to find solitude energizing and feel drained of energy when compelled to be among large groups of people for any length of time. Having said that, many extroverts enjoy the solitude of retreat and find it refreshing and energizing, and some introverts find themselves uncomfortable in the deep solitude of a silent retreat.

It can therefore happen that a person embarks upon a silent retreat only to discover that the solitude feels oppressive. Occasionally, people experience real difficulty with the solitude.

One of the blessings, and the safeguards, of an individually given retreat is that you will always have a companion who is deeply committed to looking after you while you are on retreat. This is part of what is expected of a retreat guide. It is, in part, a ministry of hospitality. So if it all becomes overwhelming, and you want to flee from the silence, talk it through first with your guide.

There are a number of reasons this can happen. The most common reason is that the silence can reveal an emptiness, or an aching, or some truth that we would rather not know about. You and your guide together may be able to look at this possibility and decide on the best course of action, whether to move gently into the source of the problem or leave things as they are.

It may be that other, more external matters are troubling you and disturbing the fruitful potential of your solitude.

Difficulties that you have left at home, such as family problems, may be haunting your retreat. Again, talk it through with your guide. Don't suffer in silence. Sometimes problems of this nature can be resolved by a well-timed phone call. Sometimes they need exactly the kind of distance that a retreat affords. You will make your own decisions. Your guide can help with this kind of discernment and will offer you the moral support that you need.

It may be that your personality simply reacts badly to solitude in ways that you couldn't have predicted. If, having talked it through with your guide, you decide that you really don't want to make this silent retreat after all, remember always that you are a free being and can leave at any time. No one will pressure you to stay in a situation in which you feel uncomfortable, and no one will think any less of you if you make this decision.

If the "prayer time blues" come over you in a sudden wave of despondency, let your guide know at once. Most guides in a residential retreat will make themselves available at odd hours of the day or night if there is a genuine need. Normally a guide will be vigilant in sensing this kind of desolation, possibly even before you are aware of it yourself.

This kind of problem is very rare, and the vast majority of people find their time in solitude extremely fruitful. Most retreatants realize that their solitude is actually being held in a warm and loving, though mainly wordless, companionship.

PRACTICALITIES TO CONSIDER

What will you need on retreat?

Very little will be needed for a daily-life retreat. It may be useful to bring a Bible to each meeting with your guide. Keep a notebook and pencil handy throughout the retreat to make a note of the guide's suggestions for prayer and to remind yourself of any thoughts, feelings, or reflections you may wish to share with your guide at your next meeting. Many people keep regular prayer journals by taking a few minutes at the close of each prayer time to consciously take note of what has happened and to make a brief record for future reference.

For any residential retreat the following checklist may be helpful:

• Casual, comfortable clothes that make you feel at home. There's no need to take half the wardrobe with you, but it is important that you feel at ease in whatever you do take.

• Sandals or comfortable shoes for use in the house.

• Good walking shoes or hiking boots, if the retreat house is situated in an area where it is possible to go for country or seaside walks. If in doubt, err on the side of assuming that you will need these. It can be very disappointing to arrive in a place where the great outdoors is beckoning you, but you have no suitable shoes in which to explore it.

• Warm, weatherproof outdoor clothing, if you are hoping to go for walks.

• Personal toiletries. Most houses provide towels and linens, but if there is any doubt about this, check before you go.

• A Bible, notebook, and pens or pencils. You may also want to bring some colored pencils or markers and a drawing pad.

• Any meditation aids that you would like to have with you. Note, however, that the use of candles may not be permitted because of the fire risk. Check with the retreat-house administration before you use candles in your room.

• An alarm clock. This may sound like the last thing you think you want with you on retreat, but it can be helpful to know that if you want to be awake in time for breakfast, morning prayer, or an early meeting with your guide, you won't miss it by oversleeping. You don't have to set it, of course, if you don't need to, but just knowing that it is there may actually help you to sleep better.

And a few things you won't be needing . . .

Books. Reading can be quite a significant distraction, especially during an individually given retreat. It can seriously deflect you from the path God is inviting you to walk with him. However, I personally always take some poetry with me, to read outdoors when the sun shines or to ponder before falling asleep. If you must read, try to do so only for the purpose of relaxation. Don't be tempted to use your retreat as a time to study some aspect of theology or to catch up on the current best-seller. Give the time to God and trust God to use it wisely and in your own best interest.

Elaborate clothing. You won't be going to any dinner parties or dining at the captain's table. Just take what you need to feel comfortable. Traveling light can be a spiritual statement as well as an easier way to make a journey.

High-tech accessories, such as your laptop computer, your radio-cassette player, or your mobile phone. As with all things, of course, the exception proves the rule. You may find, for example, that listening to gentle music on your Walkman helps you to relax. You may feel you need your cell phone in case there is an urgent need to contact home. However, cell phones can often be distracting to their owners and annoying to other people. This will be especially true in the atmosphere of a retreat house. Most retreat houses will have a pay phone and will also take incoming phone messages, especially in the case of an emergency. Try as hard as you possibly can to leave all traces and reminders of your work behind you when you set off for your retreat, and *insist* that your coworkers leave *you* alone for the duration. In a silent retreat, experience the silence as fully and deeply as you can.

Your walking shoes, Bible, and notebook are packed securely in your overnight bag. The sitter has been secured, and tomorrow's dinner is tucked away in a casserole in the refrigerator. All set? Let's go!

i'm here! now what?

YOUR TIME OF PREPARATION is over and the day has arrived. Most retreat houses encourage retreatants to arrive around midafternoon to give them time to settle in before the retreat proper begins in the evening. And so, you set out in plenty of time to arrive at your chosen retreat house for your first individually guided retreat. When you do arrive, what are you going to find there?

First, you will be welcomed. You will probably find this the kind of welcome you would receive when visiting a friend's house. A member of the retreat team or the household will meet you, greet you, and show you to your room. You will probably be invited to relax with a cup of tea or coffee, and you may be shown around the house. It can feel like the first day at school, and you may worry that you will never find your room again if you ever leave it. Be assured

that after the first day you will be feeling at home, and
nobody will ever mind your asking for help or directions.

FIRST THINGS

In your room, or on a notice board, you will find the house
schedule and any other information you need to feel comfortable and at ease. For an individually given retreat, the
timetable will usually consist of nothing more complicated
than the mealtimes and the times of any shared worship.
The rest of the day is yours to do with as you like.
However, if you are making a retreat in a religious house
where you have chosen to participate in the daily life of the
order itself, you will be expected to attend the daily office
or other services that shape the day of the community. In
this situation, there will be a strict delineation of night and
day, and you will be told the necessary arrangements and
details of timing at the beginning of your retreat.

Remember that absolutely everything is optional.
When you entered the door of the retreat house, you did
not take permanent vows! You are there to meet God in
your own way, and the routine of the house will help you
do this. You are free to come and go and to join in worship as you wish. All that might be asked is that you let
the kitchen staff know if you are going to miss a main
meal. If you enjoy some physical activity, the retreat house
will probably not refuse help with the garden, but you
could just as well take a walk or use a swimming pool or
exercise room if available.

Whether you are a night owl or early bird, in most residential retreats your days and nights will be yours to arrange as you wish, more or less. Thankfully, the kingdom of heaven has plenty of mansions, with rooms for the night owls and the early birds and all variations in between. And while a retreat house isn't exactly the kingdom of heaven, it does—or should—try to operate on the same principles. Within the constraints of mealtimes, teaching sessions you may be attending, or meetings with your retreat guide, you will be free to set your own schedule and to vary it as you wish. The only restriction on this overall freedom is that you avoid disturbing anyone else. Get up at 6:00 A.M. if you wish, but don't wake the neighbors.

You may be surprised to discover how quiet a retreat house becomes after 10:00 P.M. (or sometimes even earlier). The night silence must be observed for the sake of all other guests and residents, but there will usually be a little beverage station where you can make yourself tea or coffee at any time of the day or night, provided you do it quietly. It should also be possible for you to wander around in order to read in a sitting area, to use the chapel or other places for prayer, or just to relieve your insomnia. When you are on retreat, you are simply living in a bigger family than usual; the same guidelines for courtesy apply.

People occasionally find that the experience of being on retreat alters familiar sleep patterns—usually for the better. Habitual night owls may discover, to their benefit, that the hours before midnight may be used for sleeping. Habitual late risers may learn that the joy of daybreak is

sometimes worth waking up for, while overtired early
starters relish the extra hour or two under the covers. All
things are possible with God, especially in retreat!

The first evening

If you are part of a group making a retreat at the same
time, on the first evening of your retreat there will probably be an opportunity for you to gather together before
the silence begins. This is a chance to meet and get to
know the people who will be accompanying you.

Typically, one retreat guide (or retreat director) will
accompany as many as five or six retreatants during the
week. Often your guide will arrange a short meeting with
the five or six of you on the first evening. Sometimes this
meeting will include a time of quiet prayer together or a
chance to introduce yourselves and arrange the times for
the daily meetings between the guide and the retreatants.
If this is your first retreat, inform your guide of this fact so
that he or she will make sure that you feel at ease. If anything at all comes up during the week, whether deeply
spiritual or completely practical, your guide is the first
point of contact. He or she is there to make sure that any
problems are resolved and that your quiet is undisturbed
as far as is humanly possible.

Once the initial meeting is over, the silence usually
begins, perhaps at about 8:00 or 9:00 on the first evening.
From that point on you will be asked to respect the
silence within the house and its gardens. This is not an
imposition or even a discipline but a *gift* that retreatants

offer each other. Often a silent retreat brings people into contact with the deeper reaches of themselves and their life issues. If another person interrupts this encounter, the process is disturbed.

Mealtimes in silence are not as problematic as you might fear. Very often, gentle background music accompanies the main meals, and the silence at table is friendly, cooperative, and companionable. You will be surprised at how much can be communicated without words, and you may begin to be more lovingly observant of others, and they of you, than you would have believed possible. This nurturing silence prevails throughout the house and is communicated by smiles and gestures that help people to become more—not less—aware of each other's needs. You can also exercise a kind of benign neglect if you see that one of your companions is very preoccupied or turned inward. Allowing them a neutral space in which to stay close to their own process can be a great gift.

The retreat begins

Now that you are alone in the silence, the days are yours to shape as you will. The routine of mealtimes, worship, and the daily meeting with your guide help to structure the day, but you may still be surprised to find how hard it can be at first to use your time well. Your guide will be glad to help with this, if you ask, and will give you guidelines on finding a balance between rest, prayer, and recreation. Plan space for all of these things.

A time of retreat is a time to rest, and if you feel
tired, don't be afraid to lie down and sleep! God can
speak to your heart just as effectively (and perhaps more
so) when you are asleep as when you are awake. Times
of prayer can also be planned. Your guide may suggest
ways of incorporating prayer periods into your day and
help you to decide how often, and for how long, you
should pray.

Closeness to God is not, of course, limited to periods
of deliberate prayer, and you will probably sense a deepening into God in everything you do. Enjoy the peace
and the space. Savor the food and take advantage of the
surrounding countryside. Use your senses to help you
grow in awareness of everything around you. In a retreat,
you really do have the time to stand and stare, as well as
to touch, taste, and feel. Make the most of it. You will be
amazed at what you notice; in everything God is waiting
to greet you in some way.

Meeting with your guide

You may feel apprehensive about the time with your
guide. Remember, your guide is there just to be alongside you as a listening friend who is completely *with* and
for you. The real guide is the Holy Spirit. Your retreat
companion is a privileged bystander who will help you
to discern God's action in your prayer and your life. He
or she will do this primarily by reflecting back to you
those things that seem to be touching you deeply. The

daily meeting will normally not last longer than half an hour. It is open space in which you can share as much or as little as you wish.

Taking notes throughout the day will not only make you more aware of what is happening but will also help you remember certain topics that you may wish to bring up in your meeting. Keeping track of whatever comes to your attention as you move through the day will help you to make the most of both your own time and the time you spend meeting with your prayer companion. Remember that your guide will probably be accompanying several other people each day, so it is not a good idea to bring up the most important issue in the last two minutes of your meeting.

At the end of your meeting, the guide will normally suggest a focus for the next day's prayer, based on what you have shared. This will often be a passage of Scripture, but may also be other material, such as a poem, a picture, or some form of prayer exercise—whatever your guide feels might be helpful to you personally. This does *not* mean that you are obliged to use this focus. Every retreat guide would assure you that you should follow the prompting of the Holy Spirit in your own heart rather than adhering blindly to their suggestions. Any suggestions the guide offers are merely meant to help you move forward. Most frequently, a guide's suggestions will provide you with a useful starting point, and the Holy Spirit will draw you along from there in the way that will be most beneficial to you.

Taking time to relax

In any retreat, the hoped-for encounter with God and with our deepest and truest self happens most readily when we are relaxed and receptive, free of preconceptions about God, God's will, and our own performance. Relaxation is thus built into the process. The first relaxation is in our approach to prayer—in letting God be God to us and in us rather than in trying to achieve some kind of success in prayer. Second, there is relaxation from our normal, and often stressful, daily schedules.

The shape and form of this second kind of relaxation during a retreat depend on the type and the duration of the retreat. Most people who sign up for a one-day event, a quiet day, or a theme day are looking for some nourishment in their spiritual life, and they will often be looking to the retreat guide to provide it. A good retreat leader, however, will always remain aware that God alone provides this longed-for nourishment. The facilitator will only offer a backdrop for the search for that sustenance, a few pointers to help the retreatants to focus their hearts and minds in a particular direction. Then time will be set aside for each retreatant to reflect on what has been offered and to let God speak to them as individuals. This is the time to relax and listen to God, perhaps by walking outdoors, sitting beside a window or lake, or simply closing our eyes and resting in the peace of this oasis space. It would be reasonable to expect at least a couple of hours during a quiet day for this kind of time-out.

In a longer theme retreat, this kind of pattern will recur day by day. Evening activities, such as a time for being together socially with other retreatants, might be arranged purely for relaxation purposes. Some retreatants report that they valued the free time very highly and would have liked more of it. Others actually find it difficult to relax and to fill in the available leisure time fruitfully. Certainly some theme retreats are more structured and full than others. If you are looking specifically for a more structured form of retreat, it is worth asking the organizers for a little more detail about the shape of the days before you book a place.

In an individually given retreat, what each person does in the way of relaxation will be determined individually, often in consultation with the prayer companion. It is wise to allow time each day for pure recreation, during which you feel free to follow your nose with no conscious attempt to pray or reflect. You will discover, however, that the reflective process is a continuous one that will be enhanced and enriched by your taking time simply to be.

You may feel the desire to fill up your free time in an individually given retreat by reading books. If so, talk the matter through with your retreat guide. Reading (even "spiritual" reading) can become a serious distraction from whatever God is wanting to open up to you in your prayer, and it sometimes offers us an unconscious excuse to avoid things within us that we could be looking at in prayer. The same thing applies to writing letters, or making lengthy phone calls, or watching television—all of which have the potential to distract us in a negative way.

Your retreat guide will help you to discern what might be helpful to you and what might be a distraction. Physical exercise, however, especially if it involves walking in a garden, in the countryside, or along the seashore, can be both relaxing and conducive to reflection.

In a really long silent retreat (more than eight days), definite days of rest or repose will be scheduled. On these days you will be free to take the day off if you wish, and possibly to talk with other retreatants.

MAKING THE MOST
OF YOUR RETREAT EXPERIENCE

Perhaps your retreat will comprise just a single day of quiet, reflective time, or it may be that you are fortunate enough to get away for several days or even weeks. Whether it is happening amid the stress of everyday life or in the seclusion of a retreat house, you will want your retreat to be as fruitful as possible and a source of nourishment for a long time to come.

How can you help this to happen, given that prayer is a gift and not something any of us can achieve? We might look at a few ways of making your day(s) of quiet as rich in blessing as possible.

Stop worrying

Whenever I make a journey, I find myself going over and over in my mind all the things I may have forgotten. This usually carries on until I have passed the halfway mark of the journey and realize that whatever I've forgotten is no longer worth going back for. I can then focus my attention on what lies ahead rather than on what I have left behind.

In a retreat, you will be leaving quite a lot behind. In a residential retreat, this will include your work, your family, your friends, your duties, and the expectations that others impose upon you. This is a rare treat, and one that will not last forever—so make the most of it. Your colleagues, believe it or not, will be able to carry on in your absence; your family will continue to eat, dress themselves, and go about their normal routines. You have made all the necessary arrangements, so now is the time to enjoy the freedom.

In a retreat in daily life, this sense of freedom comes in smaller packages: the time you have given over to prayer each day and the time for meeting your guide. These times, too, are freedom times just for you and God to share.

To stop worrying is much easier said than done; nevertheless, once your retreat has begun, there is nothing more you can do to ensure that life continues while you are away, so you might as well relax your hold. This is the first hurdle of trust. Of course, if real anxieties or emergencies should arise during your retreat, you will need to attend to them, but you will not be on your own. Your retreat guide and other members of the retreat-house community will do everything they possibly can to help you resolve whatever comes up. Routine family squabbles or problems in the boardroom or on the shop floor, however, should *not* be allowed to count as emergencies.

Find and maintain a routine

While you were still planning your retreat, you may have worked out just how and when you would make the time for prayer and reflection. During a quiet day or a quiet weekend, this will generally be fixed for you. The retreat leader will have worked in some time for private prayer, and you will simply use the time to focus on anything that particularly spoke to you during the preceding talk, allowing your prayer to lead you where it will.

In a retreat in daily life, be continually aware, day by day, of how long you originally intended to pray each day. The length of time is less important than the discipline of staying faithful to what you have decided. Often prayer comes alive at the end of a period set aside for it. If you get bored halfway through and cut the time short, you may be missing the very grace for which you have been praying. Being faithful to the time we give to God in prayer is also a way to deepen our relationship with him.

If you find that your original hopes about when and where to make your prayer time are not working out in practice, it might be worth sitting back quietly and reviewing the situation, possibly talking it through with your prayer companion and making changes if necessary. It may also be worthwhile to reflect on the *reasons* your intentions are failing. Sometimes there are objective reasons, practical matters that we can do little to change. If this is the case, try to work around them, settling on a more helpful time and place for prayer.

At other times, our reluctance to pray lies in ourselves, our unconscious fear of what the silence may uncover. If you sense that this may be the case, the need to honor the time you have decided on is especially important, and it may also be helpful to talk through these feelings with your prayer companion/ prayer guide.

In a residential retreat, you will need to give some structure to your days. In a theme retreat, the timing of the input or teaching sessions will usually impose some structure. In an individually given retreat, the structure of the day is largely yours to determine. Your retreat guide will be able to help you plan for prayer times during the day.

You will certainly benefit most from your time in retreat if you can arrange your days to include each of the following aspects:

• Intentional periods of prayer

• Reflection on your prayer

• Relaxation

• Exercise

• Shared prayer or worship with the other retreatants and the community

Engage the created world

Your retreat should be an experience of wholeness; a retreat is for your body as well as for your mind and soul. The retreat house will look after your needs for nourishment and will probably offer suggestions about walks and rambles beyond the retreat-house grounds. It is up to you to make the exercise happen and—above all—to *enjoy* it.

These days in retreat are a rare opportunity to really engage the created world around you. There is time for whatever you want to do. I know of someone who went for a walk along a country lane during a retreat and stopped to gaze at the life going on in a tree at the roadside. He has no idea how long he had been standing there, reflecting on all he was seeing, before he became aware that a car was waiting patiently to get past him on the narrow road!

So, without causing traffic jams, take this God-given opportunity to notice what is happening, moment by moment, among all of God's creatures. Allow yourself to reconnect gradually to the deeper wholeness that underlies all our apparent separateness. Use all your senses. Notice the shifts in the weather, the changing patterns of the clouds, the movements of the wind, the varying shades of light throughout the day, the clarity of the stars, the phases of the moon. You will be surprised at how deeply God can speak to your heart through the simple awareness of the living world. I find that a reflective walk like this each day is an invaluable part of a retreat, as well as being a simple delight for its own sake. If walking isn't easy for you, or if the weather is less than friendly, spend some time at your window, letting the view enter your soul and speak its meanings to you.

During a retreat in daily life, it is also worth taking a little extra time at some point during each day to be present to the created world.

• Walk through the garden or spend a few minutes in the park.

• Take a few moments to gaze at your sleeping child or sit with an elderly relative.

• Just be with your cat or dog and appreciate all that makes them so wonderfully "other."

• Arrange a few flowers more purposefully than usual, or reflect on what you are really doing when you prepare the family meal.

• Take five minutes away from the office, even if all you can do is walk around the parking lot.

• Spend a little extra quality time with a friend, a partner, or your children.

A relaxing hour in a coffee shop or the preparation of a special meal can be just as much a part of your retreat in daily life as the time you have set aside for prayer—these things are all drawing your focus beyond the boundaries

of your own kingdom to the ways in which God waits to
be discovered in the world around you.

How Shall I Pray?

Everyone who seeks God prays a little differently. Use
whatever approach to prayer you find most helpful, and
"pray as you can, not as you can't." However, often during a
time of retreat, new ways of prayer offer themselves, and you
may feel drawn to pray in ways you haven't tried before.

If this is something that interests you, talk to your
guide about new approaches to prayer. Your guide may
suggest new possibilities, not because there is anything
wrong with how you normally pray, but simply to open
up new doors for you. A time of retreat can be an ideal
opportunity for exploring the possibilities of imaginative
meditation or praying with Scripture, for example. Some
suggestions for further reading on the subject of prayer
are included in appendix 2.

Reflect on your prayer

An essential component of prayer, especially during
retreat, is the reflection *after* a period of prayer on how
you were feeling *during* the prayer: what movements you
noticed within yourself, what the prayer seemed to be
about, and where it might be leading.

All too often in normal daily life, there is precious little
time for prayer in itself, let alone for reflecting on the

effects of prayer. In retreat, things are different. There *is* time. You have cleared some space in your life to *make* time. Whether you are making your retreat in daily life or in seclusion, the importance of this kind of reflection cannot be overstated. It is a way of gathering the fruits of a time of prayer and of incorporating them into your life.

The purpose of this kind of reflection is to increase your awareness of the ways in which God is active in your life and of your own response to that activity. Things to consider during a period of reflection might include the following:

• *How did I feel during this time of prayer?* Was I in harmony with myself and with God, in a kind of inner resonance, or was I feeling disturbed, uncomfortable, or distracted? Was I tuned in to the core of my being or was there a lot of interference? Did the time pass quickly, or was I struggling to stay with it? Don't make any judgments about your observations. Simply be aware of them, and maybe share them with your prayer companion. These different nuances of feeling during a time of prayer, followed by some reflection on what may have been the root cause of those feelings, can be a help in discerning what is drawing you closer to God and what is pulling you away.

• *Did anything particularly strike me in what I was using as a focus for my prayer?* Something may have stood out from a passage of Scripture, an imaginative contemplation of a Gospel scene, or a look back over the events and reactions of the past day. Just notice anything that caused a reaction in you, whether it seems positive or negative. A strong reaction in any direction is a sign that your psyche (where the Holy Spirit is indwelling) is signaling interest in something and nudging you with an invitation to look at this point more deeply, perhaps by taking it back into your next period of prayer.

• *Can I make any connections between what has come up in my prayer and what is happening in my life, or in the life of the world I live in?* One of the most potent gifts, especially of scriptural prayer, is being led to discover connections between the actions and values of God and the events and demands of our own daily lives. When we start to make these connections and to live out their conse-quences, then prayer really starts to make a difference.

• *Did the prayer leave me enlightened or challenged in any par-ticular way?* Be specific and make a note of what you find. A feeling of discomfort around some issue, for example, may be an invitation from God to make some necessary change of attitude or action. A period of prayer that has been experienced as deeply peaceful may have opened up new perspectives and insights for you or helped you to deepen your awareness that you truly are a loved child of God and a cherished part of God's creation.

• *What was the one most significant aspect of the prayer?* For what gift, granted in the prayer, do I most wish to thank God? Is there one thing I would like to go back to or carry with me into my day?

• *What do I want to share with my prayer companion from this period of prayer?* Again, make a note of any points that you want to bring up at the next meeting with your guide. This helps in two ways: it encourages you to be more aware of what was really most significant for you in the prayer, and it helps you to make the best use of the time with your guide.

Pace yourself

A retreat can be a much longed-for time of withdrawal, bringing with it the temptation to pack in as much prayer as is humanly possible. This temptation may need to be resisted. The longer the period of retreat, the greater the need to pace yourself to avoid spiritual and physical exhaustion. A weekend retreat may be something of a fast sprint; an eight-day retreat is more like a middle-distance run; a thirty-day retreat is definitely a marathon. If you try to run a middle-distance race at the speed of a fast sprint, the results will disappoint you, as every athlete knows. Take time to relax, to reflect, and to keep a balance in your days.

Sleeping and Dreaming

If you are making a residential retreat, this may be a rare opportunity to catch up on some sleep or even to break a poor sleep pattern. You are on retreat. It's okay to sleep longer in the morning if you wish, to have an afternoon nap, to go to bed as early or as late as you wish. Many guides will encourage you to wind down and rest for the first couple of days of a retreat. Prayer does not come easily to the person who is exhausted, and many people come into retreat in a seriously exhausted state.

We hear God's Word in our hearts and feel his touch upon our lives most readily when we are rested, relaxed, and receptive. Sometimes he needs to "switch us off" so as to get his word in edgewise. Indeed I have come across people who have been struggling for years to deal with some problem in their lives, and a whole new perspective has opened up when they were off guard, or even fast asleep!

This brings us to dreams. You may dream more in retreat, or rather, you may be more mindful of your dreams. Notice them and feel free to share them with your guide. They may be another way in which God is speaking within you. Dreams can sometimes be extensions of your waking prayer or provide a point of entry for your next intentional prayer time.

One woman told me of a particularly meaningful bit of personal insight she received while she was sleeping one night during a retreat:

We began with the Eucharist, which included an impromptu dramatic reading of the Passion story. Afterward, we were free to pray the Passion in our own way and in our own time. I didn't know where to begin, so I resorted to what was familiar to me: a lump of clay. During the service, some lines from an ancient hymn had been persistently on my mind: "Deep in thy wounds

Lord, hide and shelter me," and "Wash me with the water, flowing from thy side." I picked up my clay and squeezed it hard and put a slash in its side. I then made a tiny figure and tried to put it in the gash. It was too big! Food for thought: I have to become smaller or Jesus has to become bigger—the clay had already become Jesus and me! Gradually, I found myself adding to and shaping the original lump to form a recognizable torso, until a loving arm was protecting me. It felt OK.

I had been struck by the attitudes of the various people in the Passion story and wanted to explore this. During my sleep that night, I dreamed that I saw hands and arms in all sorts of gestures, and the next morning I spotted an advertisement depicting similar positions. I photocopied these and enlarged them as I knew that they were significant, but I wasn't sure how to use them. The artist, like the priest, was always at hand to offer help if needed. He scattered the pages on the floor, and they fell roughly into the shape of a cross. I'd had no intention of depicting anything so obvious as a cross! However, the rhythm of the stylized gestures made it a very powerful statement of authority and condemnation that could not be ignored. Colin, the artist, asked me if I knew that I could photocopy my hands. I experimented with various gestures and was intrigued by what emerged—the shadows, the lights, the hints and suggestions of form or substance, and the blackness, always the blackness.

These were my hands, and I put them in the form of a cross. This made a strong impact on me. These were my hands, my hidden agendas. It wasn't so much about what I'd actually said or done, but about my inner attitudes. . . . Then I looked at my first creation. I had almost come full circle. I recognized my need to be washed and sheltered deep in his wounds. I didn't want to

*do a cross, I didn't want to think about it, and yet I was drawn
there, that's where my focus was. There was light, even in the
darkness of the cross; there was hope; there was life in looking.*

ENCOUNTERING GOD
IN YOUR WORSHIP

Start each new day of your retreat with hopeful expectancy,
but without any prejudgments. You might like to begin
each morning with a short time of prayer, committing the
day and all its surprises to God, asking God to direct every
particle of your being toward himself and giving back to
him the minutes and hours of the day to use as he will to
deepen your relationship with him.

God's presence can surprise us at different times and in
different ways, and for many retreatants the context of
communal worship is one of these ways. In some of the
larger centers, a daily Eucharist is celebrated and is regarded
as a pivotal point in the day. Often, a time for silent
shared prayer is also set aside, either in the morning or
in the evening.

Where daily acts of worship are celebrated, attendance
is optional. However, most people who make retreats find
themselves drawn to share in worship with the other
retreatants and with the community living in the house.
For some, the opportunity for regular worship (which
may also include the daily office in a religious community) turns out to be an unexpected joy.

In smaller centers, a daily Eucharist may not be possible, but an opportunity for shared prayer usually will be, and there will always be a chapel or similar room where all can gather for prayer. At times when group worship is not being conducted, these sanctuaries are also available for individual prayer and reflection. Although it is certainly not necessary to be in church to pray, there are times when such a location can be particularly helpful.

In an individually given retreat, oases of shared worship are an opportunity for the individual retreatants to come together in prayer, reminding each of them that they are all part of a much greater whole.

In a theme retreat, the retreat leader will often suggest a time of shared praise and worship, which may include morning or evening prayer. Sometimes these occasions will be silent and contemplative, and sometimes they will be vocal and exuberant. This depends a great deal on the Christian tradition(s) of the house and of those who are present. I have two lovely memories of such events. One is of a day of reflection in the East End of London, among a mix of predominantly Cockney and Caribbean men and women who broke into song quite spontaneously at one point in our prayer. Another is of a retreat in Dublin in which the Sunday Mass was wonderfully enlivened by the magical harmonies of traditional prayers sung by the retreatants in the Irish language.

If you are making a residential retreat in which a daily Eucharist or other form of worship is celebrated, your retreat guide may ask you to contribute to that worship on one or more of your days there. You may be invited to read, for example, or to bring up the offertory gifts, or to serve as a eucharistic minister. You are free, of course, to decline, but don't let your nervousness take over. This type of sharing is a way of ministering to your fellow retreatants and is not nearly as threatening as it may at first appear.

If daily worship is an important factor in your choice of a retreat, it is worth asking beforehand what the house arrangements are.

GOING HOME: TIME TO REFLECT

Over the days of your retreat, you probably discovered your own rhythms of rest, exercise, and prayer. As this happened, you began to notice that God's encounters with you evolved during this special time. Let God be God, whatever is happening in your prayer and reflection. Some retreats are remembered in years to come as mountaintop experiences ripe with new insights and direction. Others are recalled as gentle times of quiet, of simply being in the silence with God. Others, again, can be times of challenge and even of painful new growth. Trust God in all that is happening, and entrust yourself to God's leading.

On the final morning of a full six- or eight-day retreat, you may find the chatter at breakfast quite disturbing after the days of silence. Or you may welcome it as a needful transition between the retreat situation and your home routine. It may be hard to leave, or you may be glad to return to the world beyond the retreat-house doors. Whatever your feelings, only the weeks, months, and years ahead will reveal the fruit of what has been sown in your heart during these days of intensive prayer.

The next chapter suggests some ways to prolong your retreat experience once you have returned to your regular routine. For now, simply take care as you journey home, especially if you are driving. The sudden transition from complete peace to the stress of city traffic can be a little traumatic. Drive slowly at first and give yourself plenty of space. Your reactions may not be as sharp as normal in this changed situation. When you arrive home, you may find it helpful to adjust gradually, perhaps by giving yourself some space and silence during the next few days. Having radio and television in your life again can also be a shock, so take things gently.

keeping the retreat experience alive

HOWEVER YOU FEEL when you arrive at your retreat, chances are that when your oasis time comes to an end—whether it is a day, a weekend, or six, eight, or even thirty days later—you will have mixed feelings about going back to everyday life. A common reaction to a period of retreat is simply to wish that it could continue for much longer.

However, an oasis can never be a permanent dwelling place. It was never intended to be. The whole point of the oasis is to provide rest, refreshment, life-giving water, and time for reflection in order to give new perspective, purpose, and energy to the ongoing journey. We must find ways to carry these gifts with us to the everyday world and allow those gifts to make a difference in our ongoing journey. But how?

Each retreat yields its own fruits, and only the individual retreatant will be able to say for sure (and often only in retrospect) what, exactly, has been given to the journey ahead and how this gift is to become embodied in real life choices and decisions. In reality, after a retreat we can never really go *back* to where we came from, only *forward* to the next stage in our journeying.

Here are some general principles that can help us to do just that.

Keeping prayer alive

During your retreat you will have been making time for prayer in ways that seem impossible amid the stresses of daily living. Your days of retreat have, in some form or another, been totally focused on your relationship with God. Whether your prayer has been made in formal ways at fixed times or while you were strolling through the gardens and gazing at the view or simply being wholly present to the present moment, your hours in retreat have been woven out of prayer. Going home can seem like a painful break in this pattern. You might feel that there is absolutely no chance of keeping prayer alive in that kind of way. And you would be right! As you return to the demands of job and family, neighbors and community, prayer will have to find a new space.

When I sense the hopelessness of staying close to God as I return from retreat, it helps me to reflect on the pattern of Jesus' own living. I find him, in the Gospel accounts, regularly taking time out to be with the Father in prayer, in a quiet place. I also find him, for the most part, in the thick of daily life, with crowds clamoring on all sides, begging for his touch, arguing with his position, listening, debating, and demanding.

So it seems to me, from this model, that prayer has these two faces: a small amount of time in solitude, wholly focused on the Father, and a very large amount of time spent in the bustle of the marketplace, living out what has been discovered in the time of silent solitude. Why would we expect the pattern of our own Christian living to be any other than this?

Looking at it in this way, the time we spend simply responding to the demands of daily life (which may well be more than 95 percent of our waking hours) is not a time that cuts us off from prayer but a time when the fruits of prayer are becoming incarnate in our lives, translated into real choices and real action for a real world. We may not recognize this process in ourselves, but in reality the time we spend in prayer is quietly bearing fruit in God's kingdom.

It is important to honor both aspects of the reality of prayer in this way: to make time for some silence and solitude, some time alone with God, and then to let the fruits of that time spill over into everything we do. In practical terms, we might approach this challenge in two ways:

• *By deliberately choosing to arrange our lives around some still center of prayer.* Be realistic about this. It's better to plan to spend ten minutes in prayer each day and actually do so, than to plan for an hour a day and become frustrated with ourselves because we fail.

• *By then getting on with the day,* dealing with everything that it presents to us, but seeking to grow in awareness of the many ways in which our time with God is shaping and affecting our minute-by-minute reactions and decisions. We might call this the need for ongoing reflection.

Bear in mind, too, that prayer can be a continual process, a simple daily awareness of God's presence in all that we experience. There are many more ways to pray than during our "official" prayer time. A few possibilities for discovering more expansive and flexible forms of prayer are suggested in some of the books listed in appendix 2, "Suggested Reading."

Living reflectively

We can get in touch with this dynamic process of reflection if we take a few moments each day just to call to mind what has been happening during the day. Doing this kind of exercise for a few minutes in the evening can make a huge difference to the ways in which our prayer becomes effective in our living. Everyone will find their own way of doing this reflection, but the following questions may be helpful:

• When I rerun the story of the day, what jumps out at me as being especially significant? Both good and bad

WELCOME TO
OUR STORE

00007689193   WESTSIDE MART
529 W SUMNER   HARTFORD WI

Descr.	qty	amount
<CUSTOMER COPY>		
REGU CA #04	6.441G	23.18
	@ 3.599/ G	

	Sub Total	23.18
	Tax	0.00

TOTAL   23.18
CREDIT $ 23.18

MASTERCARD $23.18
Acct/Card #: XXXXXXXXXXXX5198
Auth #: 02145Z
Ref: 5Z521044
Resp Code: 000
Stan: 0086132846

SITE ID: 7689193
CUSTOMER COPY

Earn rebates
with BP Visa
Take application
and Apply Today

THANKS, COME AGAIN
REG# 0002 CSH# 029 DR# 01 TRAN# 26262
07/13/13 09:24:07   ST#   3

```
                WELCOME TO
                OUR STORE
00007689193            WESTSIDE MART
S29 W SUMNER           HARTFORD WI


Descr.              qty           amount
------              ---           ------
            <CUSTOMER COPY>
REGU CA #04        6.441G          23.18
            @ 3.599/ G
                              ----------
Sub Total                          23.18
Tax                                 0.00
          TOTAL                    23.18
CREDIT    $    23.18


MASTERCARD   $23.18
Acct/Card #: XXXXXXXXXXXXX5198
Auth #: 021452
Ref: S52521044
Resp Code: 000
Stan: 008613284G

SITE ID: 7689193
CUSTOMER COPY

Earn rebates
with BP Visa
Take application
and Apply Today

          THANKS, COME AGAIN
REG# 0002 CSH# 029 DR# 01  TRAN# 2G2G2
07/13/13  08:24:07        ST#        3
```

memories of the day's events may come to mind. Both are equally important as potential pointers toward God's action in our lives.

• How did I react to these events or interactions? With hindsight, which of my reactions came from the deepest, truest part of myself, and which reactions came from a feeling of being driven, perhaps by my own fears or more superficial desires, or perhaps by the will of other people?

• Are there any inadequate reactions that I want to acknowledge and bring to God for healing? Is there any unfinished business that I want to commit to God? Is there anything I feel prompted to do or say tomorrow to help correct my course or to heal an injury I may have caused?

• What was the best thing that happened today? How do I want to express my gratitude for it? How might I share it so that others might have a part in its life-giving quality?

• Where was my prayer especially focused today? What has happened during the day that has connected with the hopes, desires, or dreams that shaped my prayer? Sometimes we simply don't notice the subtle ways in which God has answered prayer because we don't give ourselves time to reflect in this way.

Gradually this kind of reflection will become a habit. Eventually it will pervade all we do so that a period of reflective prayer turns into a continuous state of reflective living.

Taking time to be

The experience of retreat was an invitation to *wholeness.* It was easy in the seclusion of the retreat setting to become more aware of what helps to make us whole. When we go home, it can feel as though any trace of that wholeness has fragmented again, leaving us struggling to keep all the bits and pieces of our lives together.

Yet it needn't be so. There are many things that we can explore in our daily living to draw us back into a wholeness of body, mind, and spirit. If we can build some of these ways into our everyday routine, it will become easier to nourish the awareness and reflectiveness that lead us to the core of our being. Here are a few examples:

• *Take a little time, regularly, to reconnect to the natural world around you.* You can do this with a five-minute walk in the yard or a park or along the road to the mailbox. It might happen in a few minutes spent in silence looking at the view beyond the window, watching the sun set, listening to the rain fall, or letting yourself be in awe of the storm or the wind or the gathering clouds. In retreat, this kind of relationship with creation became almost second nature. There is no need to lose touch with it now that you are home.

• *Choose something that helps you to relax and build it into your weekly routine.* Maybe you enjoy music. If so, choose a favorite CD and listen to it with your full attention. If you enjoy reading, treat yourself to a book you haven't read and give yourself the gift of some time each week to read it. If your choice is a more active one, schedule some time on a regular basis to enjoy your favorite sport or leisure activity. All these things can help to restore perspective to the daily struggle to survive. They can also be a source of inspiration and a place to discover connections.

• *Be a bit more conscious of the food you eat, just as you were in retreat.* Turn off the television set. Linger over your food for a few minutes so that you can make the time to taste before you swallow. Encourage your senses to stay as alive as they were while you were on retreat. Notice the smell and feel and sounds of the world around you.

• *If you kept any notes of your time in retreat, reread them from time to time.* Consider keeping up this practice of writing in a journal or diary, or of expressing in drawings or symbols anything that seems to be coming up in your prayer and reflection. Don't worry if you feel you can't write or draw. These records are for your eyes only. They can become another form of prayer as new connections arise for you in the process, and the act of writing or drawing takes on a life of its own.

Turning your contemplation into action

For many people, a retreat brings to mind particular issues and may even create a specific sense of challenge. Immediately after a retreat it is well worth spending an hour or two quietly reflecting on what you feel the most significant fruits of your retreat have been. Try to answer some of these questions for yourself:

• During this retreat, what has been the one most important thing that I have learned or that God has opened up in my life? Take that one most important thing back into prayer. Perhaps you already have a sense of what it means for you and how you can take it further. If so, now would be the time to work out what you are going to do about it in practice.

• If a relationship has been coming up in your prayer, what do you feel you are being asked to do next in that relationship?

• If new possibilities have crystallized in your life, how are you going to turn them into reality?

• If an area of need in the world around you has been dominant, what role do you feel you are being asked to play in addressing that need?

• If new insights have been gained, how are you going to take them further, refine them, and perhaps communicate them to others?

• If you have made any resolutions, how are you going to implement them?

It might be a good idea to draw up a real action plan, noting quite specific ways in which you are hoping to put the gifts of your retreat into practice. But be realistic. Better, by far, to focus on just one thing you are hoping to incorporate into your life and to give all your energy to making it happen than to try to change a whole range of acts and attitudes, only to dissipate your energy and end up disappointed.

This process of reflecting on your retreat might be summed up in three simple questions:

• What have I brought away from this retreat?

• Who, or what, is it for?

• How am I going to turn it into lived reality?

The ongoing journey

Life beyond a retreat will never be quite the same as it was before, even though it can often feel as though the time in retreat is just a distant memory. To help you continue to live out the good effects of your retreat, you might like to consider one or more of the following ideas:

• Seek out the companionship of a soul friend or a spiritual director. To meet regularly with someone who will listen with loving acceptance as you share your ongoing journey is a gift that should not be underestimated. If you have made an individually given retreat, you will know the value of personal companionship in the journey of the heart. A soul friend enables you to continue to benefit from this gift in the years that follow your retreat.

• Consider joining a group of like-minded pilgrims in faith-sharing meetings. Group companionship offers enormous spiritual support and a space for growth and discernment.

• If there is a spirituality network in your area, you might like to find out what it is doing. Learn about its mission and aims, and consider becoming a part of the network yourself.

• Try exploring new approaches to prayer. Perhaps this is the time for something that was suggested during your retreat or something that you find in one of the books suggested for further reading in appendix 2.

• Keep your own spirituality grounded. Regularly check out the extent to which it interacts with the needs of the society you live in, with those in your area who are in any kind of need, or with the needs of the created world. If your contemplation is not finding some expression in action that goes beyond your individual world, it is not being fully true to the gospel that inspires it.

• Consider how you are going to seek out time at the oasis in the future, possibly by making a retreat a regular part of your life's journey.

Spiritual men and women throughout history have benefited greatly from extended periods of retreat. For the experienced retreatant who is in the process of making an important life decision, the Exercises of St. Ignatius of Loyola may be especially beneficial.

The history and purpose of these Exercises will comprise the final chapter of this book. Recognizing that few have the luxury of time needed to make a thirty-day retreat, we will look at both the extended, thirty-day form as well as the Nineteenth Annotation (daily-life form) of these Exercises.

the spiritual exercises of st. ignatius of loyola

WHY WOULD ANYONE thinking of making a retreat in the twenty-first century be interested in a Basque soldier who lived over five hundred years ago? In fact, St. Ignatius, born Iñigo Lopez, was largely responsible for a great deal that goes on in most individually given retreats today.

Iñigo was born in 1491 in the Basque region of northern Spain, the youngest of a family of thirteen. As a young man, he was trained in the arts of chivalry and seemed set for a glittering military career. Fate intervened, however, in the form of a cannonball that shattered his leg while he was defending the fortress of Pamplona in a desperate bid to push back a French invasion. Iñigo was unceremoniously carried back across the hills to his family home in the castle of Loyola, where he spent many months in pain and boredom, convalescing from his injuries.

This sudden shattering of Iñigo's dreams, however, was the beginning of a new dream—God's dream—in his life. Inigo experienced a profound spiritual conversion and decided to commit his life to God. Leaving behind his family and home in Loyola, along with his hopes of worldly glory and conquest, he set off on a pilgrimage into the unknown—a pilgrimage that in due course brought him to a place called Manresa.

Here, on the plain near Montserrat, he reflected deeply on his experience of brokenness and of how God was remaking him. He considered how he had discovered the possibility of dreaming God's dream, and the effect that was having on the inner movements of his heart and soul. During this period, living in a cave near the river, he embarked on a journey of prayer and reflection. He learned to discern God's creative action in his own heart and to distinguish this from the destructive movements he also observed within himself.

Iñigo recorded his experiences in Manresa, and the result eventually became the little book we call the Spiritual Exercises. The Exercises reveal how Inigo learned the art of discernment, as taught directly by God. In the process, Iñigo discovered the agony and the ecstasy of connecting with God's movements in his life. He also uncovered the possibility of making choices and decisions in accordance with what seemed to be God's action within him, while acting against any movements that appeared not to be coming from God.

In later years, Iñigo gathered around him a few companions who were also eager to discover the mystery of God's action in their personal living and God's direction in their life choices. Eventually these companions joined together formally and took vows to work and journey together in their spiritual pilgrimage, encouraging others to do the same. They called themselves Companions of Jesus and were the nucleus of what became the Society of Jesus, a religious order in the Roman Catholic Church, better known today as the Jesuits.

From these early beginnings, Iñigo himself led the companions through their own experience of what had happened for him at Manresa. He shared his retreat notes with them and gave them his Exercises, not as a program of education, but as a catalyst through which they might discover for themselves the power of God's Life becoming incarnate in their own living. He encouraged them, in their turn, to give the Exercises to others.

The process of discernment that Iñigo learned in Manresa became a model of discernment for the generations that followed. The first Jesuits opened up the process for many of their generation, and today's Jesuits continue to do the same. Like their predecessors, they encourage those who benefit from this particular experience to share it with others. In our generation, there has been an amazing upsurge of interest in the treasures of what is now called Ignatian spirituality The process of discernment and decision, nurtured by scriptural meditation and one-on-one companionship, has become the model for many, if not most, of the individually given retreats that are offered today.

SO WHAT ARE THE EXERCISES?

The so-called full Exercises of St. Ignatius comprise a series of meditations and reflections that would normally take around thirty days to complete in a residential setting. The meditations themselves invite the retreatant to reflect on the big questions of life, such as the following:

• What is the baseline of my existence? What is the purpose of my life?

• Where is my real security in life? Am I clinging to any false securities?

• What may be blocking my relationship with God?

• What do I really desire at the deepest level of my being? What does God desire for me?

• What movements and currents of my life are tending to lead me closer to God and to others? How can I nourish these movements and learn to work with them?

• What movements and currents in my life are tending to drift me further away from God and from others? How can I learn to act against them?

• How do I desire to respond to God's action in my life? What return would I want to make for all that has been given to me?

These questions are explored by praying the Scriptures in a personal and meditative way, seeking to make connections between a particular Gospel passage and what is happening in the life of the retreatant at a particular time. The process encourages the practice of ongoing discernment by helping the retreatant to reflect regularly on where and how God's action has been evident in the day's journeying.

Making the full Exercises of St. Ignatius usually involves four or five one-hour periods of prayer each day. Your retreat companion will help you to discover what pattern of prayer suits you best and may suggest variations on this pattern if he or she thinks it will help you. It must be said, however, that whatever pattern you choose, a retreat of this kind is an intensive undertaking that is not to be entered into lightly.

Here are the experiences of one woman who made this type of retreat:

Have you ever asked yourself the questions, "Who am I now?" "Where am I going?" and "Where is God in my life at this moment?" These were some of the questions that were around for me a few years ago when I was faced with major changes of direction in my life. It was at this time that I made the thirty-day retreat—the Exercises of St. Ignatius.

To be able to spend a month away from the busyness of my life and ministry and to have time to look again at what my call to conversion was about seemed scary and challenging yet inviting. The Exercises have their own dynamic and rhythm, and these reflections and meditations alongside selected Scripture passages

gave me the space to begin to discover what real freedom was
about. In the beginning I began to rediscover the power and the
presence of God in all of creation. There was so much I had
begun to take for granted mainly because of my involvement in
ministry and in the notion of "doing things for God." I had
time to appreciate what was around me and how everything
comes from God and is for God's glory. This in turn put me in
touch with my own vulnerability and weakness at times, but I
was constantly amazed at how God was ever compassionate and
loving—always ready to forgive and to go on loving me.

As I moved further into the Exercises, I began to discover
those things in my life that contribute to a lack of freedom in
the way I was living. The Exercises at this stage helped me to
a deeper awareness as to the choices I make and the ultimate
meaning of life. I was on this journey with Jesus, sharing in
his life and ministry while being made more aware of what it
really means to choose Jesus as my leader. I found myself
being challenged to accept who I was as God saw me. This
brought a great freedom, a sense of true identity and a basic
peace in my life. I was drawn more and more to the depths
within me, to a place of peace and love within. This was not
always a time of peace, and I experienced moments of struggle
and conflict when what I felt called to do differed from what
God was inviting me to.

There were times of emptiness and confusion too, but ulti-
mately the call to conversion was strongest, and the unfailing love
of God for me was always my source of strength. I found God
right in the center of the mess and the chaos as well as in the
more serene and peaceful moments. As the Exercises progressed,
the process of discernment in the Exercises of St. Ignatius helped

me toward clarity and vision, but it was now based on a deeper, inner conversion, and I could see that whatever I did would flow from that depth of God within me. This retreat was about finding God in everything, and it raised many challenges for me around issues of justice in the world.

This long retreat is all about God's call and the way we respond to it; it is something that has to be lived every day. The Exercises have become for me a way of life. Living them in the busy world of ministry is often very different from the thirty days I spent "on the mountain," but God is the same, and it is God's constant invitation to freedom and energy that has made my life so much more meaningful and alive. It's a day-to-day choice for me, and it's about remaining centered and focused on the things that are important. The thirty-day retreat helped me to rediscover the dream God has for me.

For those who are unable to make the full thirty-day residential retreat, the Spiritual Exercises can be made in daily life over a longer period of time, as we shall explore later in this chapter.

THE FULL SPIRITUAL EXERCISES

If you are hearing about the Ignatian Exercises for the first time, you might be tempted to pick up a book on the subject in order to do the Exercises in your private prayer time. In their printed form, the Exercises comprise a set of structured scriptural meditations, interspersed with a few very powerful nonscriptural meditations and extensive guidance on how to discern which inner movements are coming from God and which are not.

However, if you try to read the Exercises, even in their modern translations, you will not derive their full benefit and will almost certainly soon give up. The imagery and language are not readily accessible to the modern mind, and the Exercises are—and were always meant to be—an oral tradition, intended to be "given," not read. In the next few pages, you will find several options available to you that will allow you to experience the Exercises in the way that fits your particular needs.

The thirty-day retreat

To make the full Exercises in what is commonly called the thirty-day retreat or the long retreat, you will actually need to be in a retreat center for something like thirty-five or thirty-six days. This time will begin with a period of about three days for preliminary work, perhaps reviewing your own faith story with your guide and possibly with others who will be making the retreat. It will end with a winding-down period to give you space to reflect on the total experience and maybe share your reflections with the others in the group, if you are making the retreat in a group setting.

The central thirty days will be conducted in complete silence, except for your daily meetings with the guide and your participation in the daily liturgy. For about five hours each day, the retreatant will pray and reflect on the fruits of that prayer, sharing them with the guide in a daily meeting. There will also normally be three or four break days, often called days of repose, when the silence will be lifted and you will be encouraged to relax. Repose days tend to mark the end of each phase of the Exercises.

Making the Exercises like this is a rigorous and exhausting process. Ideally you will be given the freedom to proceed through the Exercises at your own pace, lingering longer with some and passing more quickly over others, depending on what is happening in your life and in your prayer. Your guide will help you pace yourself appropriately. From the beginning, Ignatius envisaged that some people would benefit from making the full Exercises from start to finish, while others would benefit most from remaining with one part or phase of the process. His approach to the giving of the Exercises was very flexible and always focused on the needs of the individual retreatant.

As with all the retreats considered in this book, the Exercises are given without any consideration of denomination. Their popularity today extends right across—and beyond—the spectrum of the various Christian traditions. To illustrate, here is one person's story about how the Exercises had an impact on her life that stretched far beyond the initial discipline.

Several years ago, after completing an intensive ecumenical two-year course on prayer, I found myself desiring prayer in an even deeper way. I experienced a hunger to listen for and hear God, for the needs of my own church as minister for prayer, as well as a desire to seek God's will for my own life. . . .

My spiritual director was a Roman Catholic nun; she gently took me through the Exercises. They were to last until Easter time the following year. I found that the ordered and structured way of prayer suited me well, and it gave me the freedom in prayer that I was seeking. My director asked me to spend an hour in prayer each day. As a Reader in the Anglican Church, I had sermons to prepare and worship leading to plan and reflect on, as well as other church and family activities. However, once I had made my commitment to prayer I found myself wanting to increase the time I spent with God.

The first stage of the Exercises journey delved to a deeper knowledge and understanding of personal sinfulness, weaknesses, and limitations. . . . From feelings of desolation came profound joy that in Jesus Christ is true healing. As each stage of the Exercises was completed, there came a clarity of vision and openness to the Spirit. This was affirmation of my faith.

In no time at all, Easter came. The final two stages of the Exercises—Christ's passion; his death and resurrection—left me with an experience of deep sorrow as I shared in his sufferings, which stirred within me a greater desire to serve and live for God. A desire to live a life grounded in God—pleasing God and enacting the desires he creates in the deepness of self. I found myself with a deeper wisdom about pain and suffering, which, little as I could have known it at the time, would be such a blessing to me later on in my own circumstances. I also learned to empathize with others' pain. This was followed by the joy of resurrection.

Vacationing in Cyprus some months later, I was reminded of how we are to find God in all things. I was walking high in the mountains with my husband. The terrain became more rocky and barren. I exclaimed, "This must be similar to Jesus in the *wilderness."* There appeared to be no living thing except our-selves, until I spotted the most beautiful bright blue flower in the barrenness, nodding in the wind.

It was breathtakingly alive. But how could it survive, I won-dered? How did it get there? Did the wind carry it? Having just completed the Spiritual Exercises, I heard it speak volumes to me, and I believe God had especially put it there to speak to me. It assured me that I would survive, no matter how rough the going might get, whatever circumstances might overtake me.

Now I accompany others in prayer myself and have discovered how wonderful it is to share with others the journey of the heart—just one way of trying to learn to love as God loves.

Individually given Ignatian retreats

In a shorter, individually given retreat in the Ignatian tra-dition (usually the traditional six-or eight-day retreat), the process is less rigorous and much more individually tai-lored to where you feel you are when you arrive at the retreat. You will probably not be aware that you are doing the Exercises in any obvious way, but it is likely that the journey of prayer that you make with your guide will be picking up something of the dynamic of the Exercises as it seems to apply to your present situation.

It is important to understand that an eight-day Ignatian retreat is not meant to be a condensed mini-version of the Exercises, but an experience of prayer that is nourished by the dynamic of the Exercises as appropriate to you at that time.

THE NINETEENTH ANNOTATION:
THE SPIRITUAL EXERCISES
IN DAILY LIFE

Not everyone who has a major life choice ahead of them has the time or the money to disappear into a retreat house for thirty or forty days. St. Ignatius was well aware of this problem; he made sure that he and his companions also offered the Spiritual Exercises in daily life. St. Ignatius suggested (and indeed used) an adaptation of his Spiritual Exercises to be made over a period of about nine months within the context of daily life and work. This form of making the Exercises is known as the Nineteenth Annotation because it is described in the nineteenth note in a set of additional notes that Ignatius includes in his text of the Exercises.

The pattern of the prayer is the same as in a thirty-day retreat, but instead of four or five hours' prayer each day for thirty days, the retreatant will normally be asked to pray and reflect for about an hour a day, and will meet the guide once every week or two over a period of up to nine months. This experience, too, is a marathon, but the fruits far outstrip even the very significant effort put into it.

The Exercises in cyberspace

Determined to integrate her spiritual journey with her everyday life, one religious sister found a new way to communicate the results of her daily prayer journey with her spiritual director—by e-mail! Of course, one cannot overestimate the value of sustained personal contact with a retreat director while making the Exercises, and yet this sister's experience is worth sharing.

For a long time I had felt that I wanted to make a thirty-day Ignatian retreat. But with my work schedule it was impossible to get away for a week. I also had a strong sense that I needed to make a retreat in my life so that I could bring together the contemplative and active dimensions of my life. I used Tetlow's binder on the Nineteenth Annotated retreat, which has instructions for both the director and directee on the retreat. Each evening I e-mailed to my director the results of my prayer experience with Scripture.

The daily accountability over six months helped me create a pattern in my life that has become a permanent gift. When I met with my director every three weeks I didn't have to "catch him up" with what had been happening on retreat. We could enter directly into exploring an important prayer experience that had been meaningful to me. Although I started the retreat, I found that God took over the direction of the retreat. Although I was more than past the time to begin the reflections on the Passion, I told my director I couldn't. Something in me wanted to stay at the Last Supper.

I began my regular eight-day retreat, which I make every year, the day after saying that to him. I read the Last Supper and was struck by the words, "You will be scandalized by me tonight." The next morning I woke up with the Agony in the

*Garden on my mind. That week of retreat I moved through the
passion and death of Jesus, profoundly moved at the love Jesus
had for me and [at] the illusions under which I was leading my
life. God himself became my director at that point as I moved
through the meditation of the Passion at his speed, not my own.
Later I picked up with the end of the Nineteenth Annotated
retreat. My life profoundly changed from those months on. When
my ministry assignment allows it, I am looking forward to making the thirty-day Ignatian Exercises.*

Making the Exercises in daily life

If you are considering making this kind of extended
retreat in daily life, you will first need to find someone
who is willing to accompany you as a guide. This is a big
commitment for both of you, and it may not be easy to
find a guide. Remember, when seeking a guide for this
particular journey, that the guide *must* have made the
journey of the Exercises, preferably individually with an
experienced director, and must be thoroughly familiar
with the dynamic of the Exercises. He or she should also
be a person with whom you feel some rapport. You are
going to be journeying together for a long time, and the
relationship between you will go deep as you share your
innermost holy ground. It is worth waiting until the right
person appears on the scene.

You would also do well to ask yourself why you actually want to make the Exercises. It would be a big mistake
to view this journey as some kind of achievement leading

to a "spiritual qualification." The end of the Exercises is always a new beginning, not a destination in itself. Your guide will be looking with you at your reasons and helping you to discern, initially, whether this is the right thing for you to do and the right time to do it.

Once you have embarked on the journey, you will need to find the time and space for in-depth prayer each day. This may mean getting up an hour earlier than usual, or sacrificing an hour of TV time in the evening to find the undisturbed time that you will need.

A few points may be worth bearing in mind:

• If you already have a soul friend or spiritual director, talk to him or her about your desire to make the full Exercises. For the duration of the Exercises, it is advisable to see only your Exercises guide on a regular basis. During the Exercises, your prayer attention will be sharply focused on the meditations offered to you each week. Talking separately to two different people during this period may lead to confusion and distraction. Your normal companion will understand this.

• In daily life, no outside discipline will be imposed on you as it would be in a retreat house. The self-discipline involved is also part of the journey. Many people discover that the commitment to prayer is bringing them such joy and such grace that they are more than happy to give the time to it. However, almost everyone will go through periods of disillusionment and dryness at some stage in the process, and if this happens, talk it through with your guide, trusting as best you can that the God who launched you into the prayer will also carry you forward until consolation returns.

• Before you think of making the full Exercises, make at least two or three shorter retreats in the Ignatian tradition, either in daily life or in residence. These will help you become familiar with the approaches to prayer and reflection that are helpful in making the Exercises. They will also help you discover whether or not this kind of journey really is for you.

• If you make a shorter individually given retreat during the period of your Nineteenth Annotation journey, do tell the retreat guide that you are currently making the Exercises. The guide will probably try to ensure that anything suggested in your retreat is compatible with where you are in the Exercises so that your overall direction is not disturbed.

The cost of making the Exercises in daily life is, of course, considerably less than a thirty-day retreat in a retreat center. Some guides will ask for a donation or fee for their time, others will not. It is important to establish from the start what your guide expects. If you visit a guide in a retreat house for your weekly or biweekly meetings, you should expect to make a financial contribution since people in this situation are doing this kind of work for a living and often have no other means of support. Most retreat houses make it clear what their

scale of expected donations is. If you are housebound, it
may be possible to find a guide who is prepared to come
to you in your own home.

The Exercises in a group setting

Another way of making the Exercises in daily life is in a
group setting. A group would not normally include more
than six people, and one guide would lead them all through
the Exercises. They would share their prayer experience
together every week or two. For many people, this is a
very fruitful way of journeying.

Bear in mind, however, that the original intention was
that the Exercises should be given one-on-one, and this
remains by far the best approach. If you have the chance
to make the Exercises in a group, you might like to ask
whether there will also be an opportunity to meet with
the group guide on an individual basis fairly regularly so
that you can explore any issues that you might not feel
happy about opening up in the full group.

Whether or not you have a specific intention or decision to make, an extended retreat—like any retreat—will
afford you the opportunity to probe the deeper questions
of life, to respond to the promptings of that indefinable
something that urges each of us at times to take a closer
look at who we are and where we are going.

I am reminded of the moment in *The Wind in the
Willows* when Mole senses that his underground home is
nearby and that it is time to return to it for hibernation. He
isn't mindful of what it is that is ruffling his consciousness,

but he knows he has to follow these unconscious urges. In the same way, we find our truest selves by responding to the nudging of our hearts, telling us that it is time to step aside and ponder awhile.

retreat centers in the united states

A FAIRLY COMPREHENSIVE LISTING of retreat centers in the United States and Canada can be found on the Web site of Retreats International in Notre Dame, Indiana (www.retreatsintl.org). In addition to the listing, the Web site contains good information about the retreat experience and a listing of books and other resources. Christian Life Community (CLC) can help you tap into a nationwide network of fellow pilgrims. See their website at www.clc-usa.org or call them at (314)977-7370.

For information on retreat centers in North America that are not included in the Retreats International listing, look at ads in diocesan Catholic newspapers and magazines. Local priests and ministers can often be helpful in locating retreat centers that will suit your needs. Contact the Cenacle Sisters through their web site to find out more about open–door retreats (www.cenaclesisters.org/nap.htm). For information on spiritual retreats in prisons, contact Mr Harry "Bud" Cope of St. Dismas Prison Ministry, 1823 Service Lane, Monesson, Pennsylvania, 15062–2317; or e-mail at budcope@att.net.

The Jesuits operate retreat houses and resource centers in a number of locations across the United States. For additional information on these houses and centers and on opportunities in other countries, consult the list on the Jesuit Web site: http://www.jesuit.org/resources/retreat.html

ALASKA

Holy Spirit Center
10980 Hillside Dr.
Anchorage, AK 99507
Phone: (907) 346-2343
Fax: (907) 346-2140
Web site:
    http://home.gci.net/~hsrh/

CALIFORNIA

Loyola Institute for Spirituality
480 S. Batavia St.
Orange, CA 92868-3907
Phone: (714) 997-9587
Fax: (714) 997-9588
E-mail: loyinst@pacbell.net
Web site:
    www.loyolainstitute.org

El Retiro San Iñigo, Jesuit
    Retreat House
300 Manresa Way
Los Altos, CA 94022
Phone: (650) 948-4491
Fax: (650) 948-0640
E-mail: retreat@elretiro.org
Web site: www.elretiro.org

COLORADO

Sacred Heart Jesuit Retreat
    House
P.O. Box 185
Sedalia, CO 80135-0185
Phone: (303) 688-4198
Fax: (303) 688-9633

FLORIDA

Manresa Retreat House
12190 SW 56th St.
     (Miller Dr.)
Miami, FL
Mailing address:
P.O. Box 651512
Miami, FL 33265
Phone: (305) 596-0001
Web site: www.efjc.com
     (in Spanish)

GEORGIA

Ignatius Retreat Center
6700 Riverside Dr., NW
Atlanta, GA 30328-2710
Phone/Fax: (404) 255-0503

ILLINOIS

Bellarmine Hall
P.O. Box 268
Barrington, IL 60011
Phone: (847) 381-1261
Fax: (847) 381-4695

INDIANA

Spiritual Life Center
1441 Hoffman St.

Hammond, IN 46327-1782
Phone: (219) 398-5047

IOWA

Creighton University Retreat
     Center
16493 Contrail Ave.
Griswold, IA 51535
Phone: (712) 778-2466
Fax: (712) 778-2467
E-mail: curc@netins.net
Web site: www.creighton.
     edu/CURC/curc.html

LOUISIANA

Jesuit Spirituality Center
St. Charles College
Grand Coteau, LA 70541-1003
Phone: (337) 662-5251 or
     (337) 662-5252
Fax: (337) 662-3187
E-mail: jespirtcen@aol.com
Web site:
     http://members.aol.com/
     jespirtcen/

Manresa House of Retreats
5858 Hwy 44
Convent, LA
Mailing address: P.O. Box 89
Convent, LA 70723-0089

Phone: (225) 562-3596
Fax: (225) 562-3147
E-mail: manresa@stargazer.net

Our Lady of the Oaks
214 Church St.
Grand Coteau, LA
Mailing address:
    P.O. Drawer D
Grand Coteau, LA 70541-1004
Phone: (337) 662-5410
Fax: (337) 662-5331
E-mail: olorhgc@bellsouth.net
Web site:
    http://members.aol.com/
    olorhgc

MARYLAND

Loyola Retreat House
P.O. Box 9
9270 Loyola Retreat Rd.
Faulkner, MD 20632
Phone: (301) 870-3515
Fax: (301) 392-0808
E-mail: reservations@
    loyolaretreat.org
Web site:
    www.loyolaretreat.org

MASSACHUSETTS

Campion Renewal Center
319 Concord Rd.
Weston, MA 02493-1398

Phone: (781) 788-6810
Fax: (781) 894-5864
E-mail: plangford@campion
    center.org
Web site:
    www.campioncenter.org

Gonzaga—Eastern Point
    Retreat House
37 Niles Pond Rd.
Gloucester, MA 01930-4499
Phone: (978) 283-0013
Fax: (978) 282-1989

MICHIGAN

Columbiere Conference Center
9075 Big Lake Rd.
Clarkston, MI
Mailing address: P.O. Box 139
Clarkston, MI 48347-0139
Phone: (248) 625-5611
Fax: (248) 625-3526
E-mail:
    columbiere@provide.net

Manresa Retreat House
1390 Quarton Rd.
Bloomfield Hills, MI 48304-
    3554
Phone: (810) 644-4933 or
    (313) 564-6455

MINNESOTA

Loyola: A Spiritual Renewal
    Resource
389 N. Oxford St.
Saint Paul, MN 55104
Phone: (651) 641-0008
E-mail: staff@loyolasrr.org
Web site: www.loyolasrr.org

The Jesuit Retreat
8243 Demontreville Trail North
Lake Elmo, MN 55042-9546
Phone: (612) 777-1311

MISSOURI

The White House Retreat
3601 Lindell Blvd., Suite 204
St. Louis, MO 63108
Phone: (314) 533-8903 or
    (800) 643-1003
Fax: (314) 533-8428
E-mail: whthouse@i-plex.net
Web site:
    http://gabrielmedia.org/whr/

NEBRASKA

Creighton University Christian
    Spirituality Program
Summer Sessions Office
Creighton University
Omaha, NE 68178

Phone: (800) 637-4279 or (402)
    280-2996
E-mail: csp@creighton.edu
Web site:
    www.creighton.edu/
    christianspirituality/

NEW JERSEY

Loyola House of Retreats
161 James St.
Morristown, NJ 07960
Phone: (973) 539-0744
Fax: (973) 898-9839
E-mail: retreathouse@loyola.org
Web site: www.loyola.org

NEW YORK

Jogues Retreat
P.O. Box F
Cornwall, NY 12518-0522
Phone: (845) 534-7570
Fax: (845) 534-3276
E-mail: joguesreat@hvc.rr.com

Manresa Retreat House
239 Fingerboard Rd.
Staten Island, NY 10305-3797
Phone: (718) 727-3844
Fax: (718) 727-4881
E-mail: skellym@idt.net
Web site: www.manresasi.org

St. Ignatius Retreat House
251 Searingtown Rd.
Manhasset, NY 11030
Phone: (516) 621-8300
Fax: (516) 621-7201

NORTH CAROLINA

Jesuit House of Prayer
289 NW US Hwy 25/70
Hot Springs, NC
Mailing address: P.O. Box 7
Phone: (828) 622-7366
E-mail: vpaul@madison.main.
     nc.us
Web site:
     www.geocities.com/~jesuit
     _housenc

OHIO

Jesuit Retreat House
5629 State Rd.
Cleveland, OH 44134
Phone: (440) 884-9300
Fax: (440) 885-1055
E-mail: jrhcleve@att.net
Web site:
     www.jrh-cleveland.org

Loyola of the Lakes Jesuit
     Retreat House
700 Killinger Road
Clinton, OH 44216

Phone: (330) 896-2315
Fax: (330) 896-0858
E-mail: lotljrh@aol.com

Milford Spiritual Center
5361 S. Milford Road
Milford, OH 45150-9746
Phone: (513) 248-3500
Fax: (513) 248-3503

OREGON

The Jesuit Spirituality Center
3400 SE 43rd Ave.
Portland, OR 97206-3194
Phone: (503) 788-6464
Fax: (503) 777-3142

PENNSYLVANIA

Jesuit Center for Spiritual
     Growth
P.O. Box 223, Church Rd.
Wernersville, PA 19565-0223
Reservations/Business Office
Phone: (610) 670-3642
General Information
Phone: (610) 670-3640
Fax: (610) 670-3650
E-mail: jescntsec@talon.net
Web site:
     www.jesuitspiritualcenter
     .org

SOUTH DAKOTA

Sioux Spiritual Center
HC 77 Box 271
Howes, SD 57748
Phone: (605) 985-5906
Fax: (605) 985-5908
E-mail:
    smitten@sioux.sodak.net

TEXAS

Montserrat Retreat House
600 N. Shady Shores
Lake Dallas, TX
Mailing address: P.O. Box 398
Lake Dallas, TX 75065-2412
Phone: (940) 321-6020 or
    (940) 321-6030
Fax: (940) 321-6040
E-mail: retreat1@airmail.net

WASHINGTON

Ignatian Resource Center
4732 18th Ave. East
Seattle, WA 98112
Phone: (206) 329-4824
Fax: (206) 726-6179
E-mail: ignatianctr@juno.com

WISCONSIN

Jesuit Retreat House
4800 Fahrnwald Road
Oshkosh, WI 54902-7598
Phone: (920) 231-9060
Toll-free from within Wisconsin:
    (800) 962-7330
Fax: (920) 231-9094
E-mail: office@
    jesuitretreathouse.org
Web site:
    www.jesuitretreathouse.org

APPENDIX TWO

suggested reading

THE SPIRITUAL JOURNEY

William A. Barry, S.J. and William J. Connolly, S.J., *The Practice of Spiritual Direction* (HarperSanFrancisco, 1982).

Margaret Guenther, *Holy Listening: The Art of Spiritual Direction* (Cowley Publications, 1992).

Kathryn Hermes, *Beginning Contemplative Prayer* (Servant Publications, 2001).

Kenneth Leech, *Soul Friend: Spiritual Direction in the Modern World* (Morehouse Publishing, 1994).

Margaret Silf, *Inner Compass: An Invitation to Ignatian Spirituality* (Loyola Press, 1998).

P R A Y E R

————, *God and You: Prayer as Personal Relationship* (Paulist Press, 1987).

————, *What Do I Want in Prayer?* (Paulist Press, 1994).

Jean C. J. d'Elbée, *I Believe in Love: A Personal Retreat Based on the Teaching of St. Thérèse of Lisieux* (Sophia Institute Press, 2001).

Anthony de Mello, *Awareness* (Image Books, 1990).

Catherine de Hueck Doherty, *Poustinia: Encountering God in Silence, Solitude, and Prayer* (Madonna House Publishing, 2000).

Meryl Doney, *The Art of Prayer: A Pathway to Spiritual Growth* (Lion Publishing, Giftlines, 1999).

Monica Furlong, *Contemplating Now* (Cowley Publications, 1971).

Thomas H. Green, S.J., *Opening to God: A Guide to Prayer* (Ave Maria Press, 1977).

Brigid E. Herman, *Creative Prayer* (Paraclete Press, 1998).

Kenneth Leech, *True Prayer: An Introduction to Christian Spirituality* (Sheldon Press, 1980).

Dennis Linn, Sheila Fabricant Linn, and Matthew Linn, *Sleeping with Bread: Holding What Gives You Life* (Paulist Press, 1995).

Margaret Silf, *Close to the Heart: A Guide to Personal Prayer* (Loyola Press, 1999).

Retreats

Jay Copp, *The Liguori Guide to Catholic U.S.A.: A Treasury of Churches, Schools, Monuments, Shrines, and Monasteries* (Liguori Publishing, 1999).

Thomas Hart, *Coming down the Mountain: How to Turn Your Retreat into Everyday Living* (Paulist Press, 1988).

Andrew Nash, *Making a Retreat* (Methodist Retreat Group, 2000).

Judy Henderson Prather, *Seeking Sabbath: A Planning Guide for Women's Retreats* (Women's Missionary Union, 1997).

Jane E. Vennard, *Be Still: Designing and Leading Contemplative Retreats* (Alban Institute, 2000).

Making a Self-Directed Retreat

Thomas H. Green, S.J., *A Vacation with the Lord: A Personal Directed Retreat* (Ave Maria Press, 1986).

Brother Ramon, S.S.F., *Seven Days of Solitude: A Guidebook for a Personal Retreat* (Liguori Publications, 2000).

Margaret Silf, *Sacred Spaces: Stations on a Celtic Way* (Paraclete Press, 2001). Material suitable for a seven- or eight-day self-directed retreat in the tradition of Celtic spirituality.

Book Series on Retreats and on Prayer

Crossroad Spiritual Legacy series, including Joseph Tetlow's Ignatius Loyola: Spiritual Exercises, pubished by Crossroad Publishing House, New York.

The series in Companions for the Journey published by St. Mary's Press, Winona, Minnesota, features volumes on praying with most of the spiritual giants in the Christian tradition.

A Retreat with . . . series, published by St. Anthony's Messenger Press, Cincinnati, Ohio. Each volume in this series provides material for a self-directed retreat with a wide variety of spiritual figures. Readers are invited in to engage in dialogue with the subject of the book.

The Fifteen Days of Prayer with . . . series, published by Liguori Publications, Liguori, Missouri. Each book in the series contains a biography of a seminal spiritual figure, a guide for setting up a format of prayer and retreat, and material for fifteen prayer periods.

More books by Margaret Silf . . .